Etsu Egami: Rainbow

The Mythenstein Project, No. 2

Martin Herb

Preface / Vorwort

3   The rainbow is a symbol of hope, peace and diversity. But it also symbolises the act of bridge-building, making it a fitting analogy for the dialogue between East and West, a dialogue that is of special importance for Japan and Switzerland in 2024. This year, we mark 160 years since our two countries first established diplomatic relations, so we have a long shared history to look back on. For this reason, I was very glad to hear that Etsu Egami, one of Japan's most interesting and important emerging artists, has been chosen for the Mythenstein Project No. 2 in this anniversary year – a truly successful example of bridge-building in the field of visual art that shows us how productive exchanges across geographical and cultural borders can be. I offer my heartfelt congratulations to all involved, with special thanks to ZWEI Wealth and Gerber & Stauffer Fine Arts for their great commitment.

Martin Herb
President, Swiss-Japanese Chamber of Commerce (SJCC)

Der Regenbogen gilt als Symbol für Hoffnung, Frieden und Vielfalt. Er ist auch ein Zeichen des Brückenschlags und repräsentiert hervorragend den Dialog zwischen Ost und West, dem 2024 für Japan und die Schweiz eine besondere Bedeutung zukommt: Vor 160 Jahren haben unsere beiden Länder diplomatische Beziehungen aufgenommen, uns verbindet somit eine lange Geschichte. Daher bin ich sehr erfreut, dass im Jubiläumsjahr mit Etsu Egami eine der interessantesten und wichtigsten aufstrebenden Künstlerinnen aus Japan für das Mythenstein Project No. 2 ausgewählt wurde. Dieser überzeugende, gelungene Brückenschlag im Bereich der visuellen Künste führt uns vor Augen, wie fruchtbar sich der Austausch über geografische und kulturelle Grenzen hinweg erweist. Ich gratuliere allen Beteiligten herzlich und danke insbesondere ZWEI Wealth und Gerber & Stauffer Fine Arts für ihr grosses Engagement.

Martin Herb
Präsident Swiss-Japanese Chamber of Commerce (SJCC)

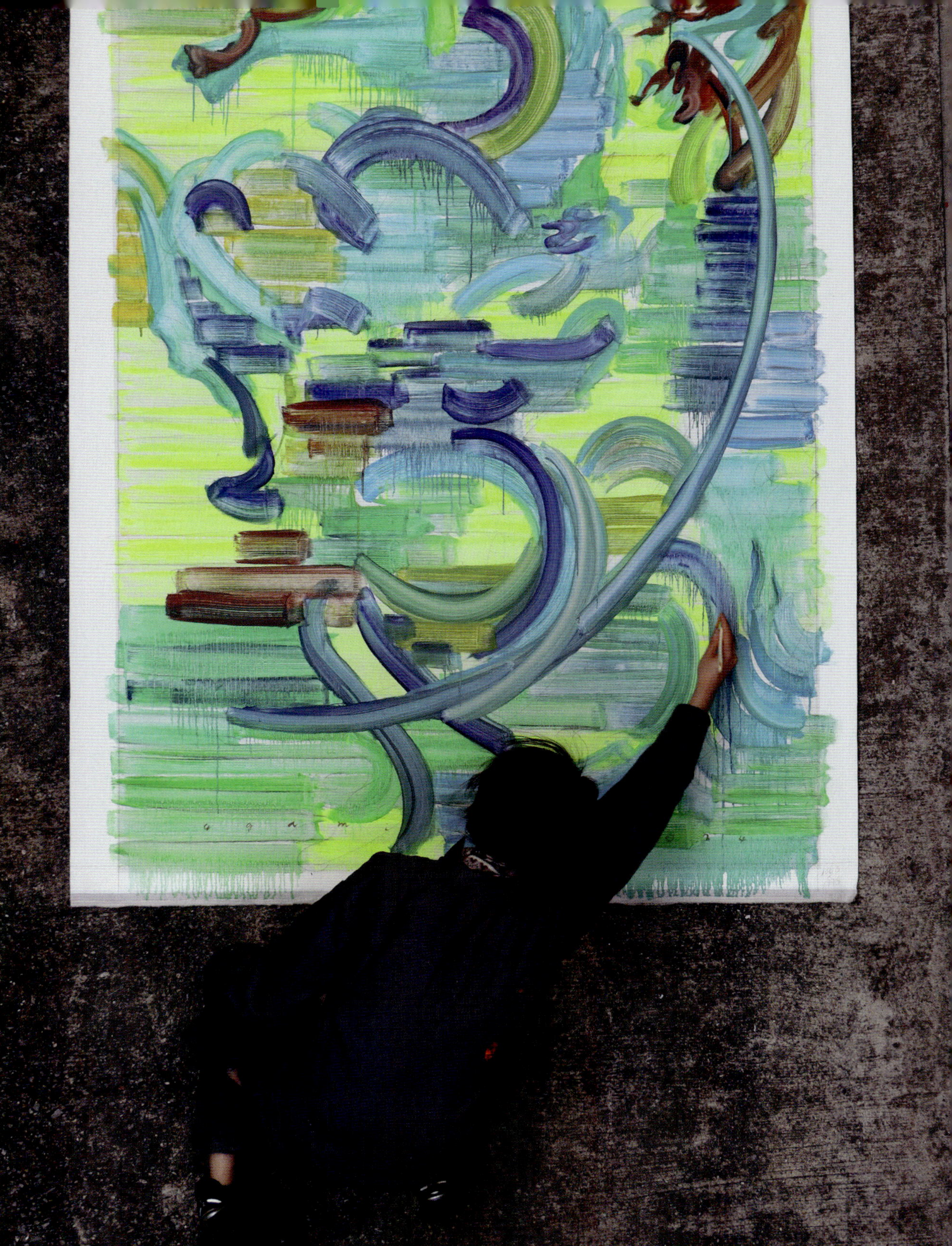

Beate Scheder

Watching the Rainbow from Afar

6   Jacques Derrida derived his neologism *différance* from the French verb *différer,* meaning both 'to differ' (to be unlike/distinct) and 'to defer' (to delay in time/postpone). He uses this concept to point to the difference between written and spoken language, a difference reflected in the word itself: phonetically, *différance* and *différence* seem the same, with the change of one letter only becoming apparent when written down. Derrida's theory of language follows on from the semiology of Ferdinand de Saussure, taking it to radical new lengths. In Derrida's view, direct communication of meaning cannot be achieved via language. Linguistic signs generate meaning only in their interplay and their distinctness from one another. As a result, meaning is in a process of perpetual change.

It is fitting that Etsu Egami cites Derrida's *différance* as a reference point for her art. She, too, is concerned with ambiguity, especially that of spoken language, and with shifts in meaning. She views language as both a form of communication and an obstacle to understanding.

Egami was born in 1994 in Chiba, Japan, and she grew up in Japan and the United States before studying at art academies in Beijing and Karlsruhe. The experience of being foreign, of coming up against the limits of language, but also of becoming entangled in misunderstandings on account of cultural differences, have been recurring themes in her life. Sometimes, as she found during her studies in China, it can be similarities that cause confusion in intercultural dialogue: although Chinese and Japanese share some of the same characters, their pronunciations and meanings are entirely different.

Egami's artistic interests are shaped by her life between cultures, focusing primarily on miscommunication and difficulties in making oneself understood due to language barriers and cultural differences. Initially, she took a multimedia approach, using primarily sound and video. For her early work, *Mishearing Game,* she asked people to intuitively interpret and pronounce words in foreign languages they were not familiar with, purely on the basis of sound.

Egami's paintings oscillate between figuration and abstraction. They could be described as a continuation of this same line of inquiry, but by other means. Her paintings are highly recognisable, in particular the coarse brushstrokes in bright colours that make up her motifs. Applied to the canvas as parallel lines, they constitute the ground over which the artist makes curving, winding gestural marks, swirling shapes in which elements of a portrait can be identified, more or less clearly, if one chooses to look for them.

On the canvas, the oil paints used by the artist appear almost translucent. The way she applies them is strongly reminiscent of the techniques of Japanese calligraphy she learned as a child. There is something almost performative about the flowing, rhythmic motion of her brush over the surface. She has said this movement is very important to her, making the pictures part of her body while she is painting them.

Movement – of the eyes, of the body, and of the mind – is also required when looking at Egami's paintings. Her compositions appear rhythmic and fluid, the colours, lines and shapes merging into one another. In some pic-

7   tures, they are clearly legible as noses, ears, eyes, mouths, cheekbones, hairlines. Others are more abstract, so that it is almost impossible to tell apart what does and does not belong to the face. When looking at Egami's painting, the eye wanders of its own accord, from side to side, up and down, and above all back and forth, because these portraits, like Impressionist paintings, require distance. If you stand too close, you see little more than brushstrokes; only when you stand back does a face take shape. The pictures need space to find their full expression. Just like people. The artist is interested not in the closeness that communication can supposedly create between individuals, but in the distance between individuals that can never be completely overcome. She translates subjective experiences into painting as a way of articulating universal questions about being together in the world.

Egami belongs to the third generation of postwar Japanese artists. In Beijing, she studied under the neo-realist painter Liu Xiaodong. Her engagement with Asian and Western art history – especially that of the Western-influenced Yōga school, which adopted the use of oil paints in early modern Japan, suddenly disappeared after World War II and was later replaced by movements like Gutai and Mono-ha – is clearly reflected in her own interpretation of the medium. The portrait is a theme to which she returns again and again, but in her own way, and which she describes as follows: "Portraying the sensibilities of Eastern people and their unique sense of perfection, but using Western means".

This approach shapes the way she sees the world: "I use the portrait to discover human nature and human instincts, recognition and miscommunication", she says. At the same time, she tries to express the ephemeral nature of beauty and of human life: "It's hard to explain – I love the cherry blossom days. The flowers are very beautiful, but they disappear suddenly, after one week or five days. I think about these things while I'm painting the human portraits."

The rainbow, too, is visible only for a fleeting moment, and also only at a distance – a meteorological phenomenon that vanishes as suddenly as it appears. Egami chose it as the title for her exhibition at Mythenstein. As well as borrowing its colours and parallel lines for her painting, she also sees the rainbow's enigmatic beauty as a symbol of the hopes and dreams that emerge amidst all the pitfalls and grey areas of communication – hope for the acknowledgement of differences between people, for peaceful coexistence and diversity.

Egami's pictures are deliberately ambiguous. She does not seek to prescribe a specific interpretation. On the contrary, what one sees in them depends strongly on the individual standing in front of them. There is no one truth, and meaning is not singular, constantly rediscovering and reinventing itself. In this sense, Egami is very close to Derrida.

Beate Scheder

Den Regenbogen von Weitem betrachten

9   Jacques Derrida leitete seinen Neologismus *différance* von dem französischen Verb *différer* ab. *Différer* bedeutet einerseits abweichen, andererseits verzögern im zeitlichen Sinne. Mit *différance* verweist Derrida auf den Unterschied zwischen Schrift und gesprochener Sprache und verdeutlicht dies schon im Begriff selbst: Phonetisch scheint es sich bei *différance* und *différence* um dasselbe Wort zu handeln, erst die Verschriftlichung macht sichtbar, dass ein Buchstabe nicht übereinstimmt. Mit seiner Sprachphilosophie schließt Derrida an Ferdinand de Saussures Zeichentheorie an, spitzt diese jedoch radikal zu. Eine unmittelbare Sinnvermittlung ist seiner Ansicht nach durch Sprache unmöglich. Nur im Zusammenspiel und in Abgrenzung voneinander erzeugen sprachliche Zeichen Bedeutung. Sinn befindet sich demnach in einem kontinuierlichen Prozess des Wandels.

Es passt gut, dass Etsu Egami Derridas *différance* als Referenz für ihre Kunst heranzieht. Diese Uneindeutigkeit insbesondere der gesprochenen Sprache und die Verschiebung von Bedeutung spielt auch für die Künstlerin eine Rolle. Bei Sprache, so legt sie dar, handle es sich um eine Form der Kommunikation und gleichermaßen um eine Hürde in der Verständigung.

Etsu Egami wurde 1994 im japanischen Chiba geboren, wuchs in Japan und den USA auf. Später studierte sie in Peking und in Karlsruhe. Es ist eine ihr vertraute Erfahrung, fremd zu sein, an die Grenzen der Sprache zu stoßen und sich darüber hinaus aufgrund von kulturellen Unterschieden in Missverständnisse zu verstricken. Mitunter – so erlebte Egami es während ihres Studiums in Peking – sind es im interkulturellen Dialog gerade Ähnlichkeiten, die in die Irre führen: In China und Japan werden zum Teil dieselben Schriftzeichen verwendet, doch unterscheiden sich deren Aussprache und Sinn grundlegend.

Egamis künstlerisches Interesse ist geprägt von ihrem Leben zwischen den Kulturen, primär befasst sie sich mit Misskommunikation und Verständigungsschwierigkeiten, die aufgrund von Sprachbarrieren und kulturellen Unterschieden erwachsen. Anfangs näherte sie sich ihrem Thema multimedial, vor allem mittels Sound und Video. Für ihre frühe Arbeit *Mishearing Game* ließ sie Menschen Wörter aus Fremdsprachen, die diese nicht beherrschen, allein anhand ihres Klangs intuitiv deuten und wiedergeben.

Egamis Malerei, die zwischen Figuration und Abstraktion changiert, ist gewissermaßen eine Fortführung der Beschäftigung mit den Voraussetzungen und Bedingtheiten von Kommunikation – nur mit anderen Mitteln. Ihre Gemälde haben einen hohen Wiedererkennungswert, auffällig sind vor allem die groben Pinselstriche in leuchtenden Farben, aus denen sich ihre Motive zusammensetzen. Parallel auf die Leinwand aufgetragen, bilden breite Striche den Hintergrund, auf dem Egami gestisch geschwungene und gewundene Linien setzt, wirbelige Formen, in denen man mal deutlicher, mal nur schemenhaft Elemente eines Porträts erkennen kann.

Als Material dient der Künstlerin Ölfarbe, die auf der Leinwand fast durchscheinend wirkt. Die Art und Weise, wie sie die Farbe aufträgt, erinnert stark an japanische Kalligrafie, die Egami als Kind erlernte. Es hat fast etwas Performatives, wenn die Künstlerin fließend, in rhythmischem Schwung den

     Pinsel über die Leinwand gleiten lässt. Diese Bewegung sei ihr sehr wichtig, erklärt sie, so würden die Gemälde beim Malen zu einem Teil ihres Körpers werden.

Bewegung – der Augen, des Körpers und des Geistes – ist auch notwendig bei der Rezeption ihrer Bilder. Rhythmisch und fluide muten ihre Kompositionen an. Die Farben, die Linien, die Formen gehen ineinander über. In manchen Gemälden sind sie klar lesbar, als Nasen, Ohren, Augen, Münder, Wangenknochen, Haaransätze. Andere Werke erscheinen abstrakter, kaum bestimmen lässt sich dort, was noch zu dem porträtierten Kopf gehört und was nicht mehr. Der Blick beginnt bei der Betrachtung von Egamis Malerei wie von selbst zu wandern, hin und her, auf und ab, vor und insbesondere zurück, denn die Porträts benötigen, ähnlich den impressionistischen Gemälden, Distanz. Steht man zu dicht vor ihren Bildern, sind in erster Linie die Pinselstriche zu erkennen, erst von Weitem formieren sich diese zu Gesichtszügen. Die Werke benötigen Raum, um sich entfalten zu können. Wie dies eben auch bei Menschen der Fall ist. Was Egami interessiert, ist gerade nicht die Nähe, die Kommunikation zwischen Menschen vermeintlich zu schaffen vermag, sondern vielmehr die Distanz zwischen Individuen, die nie ganz überwunden werden kann. Die Künstlerin übersetzt subjektive Erfahrungen in Malerei, um universelle Fragen des gemeinsamen In-der-Welt-Seins zu formulieren.

Egami gehört der dritten Generation japanischer Nachkriegskünstler*innen an. Sie hat Kunsthochschulen in Asien und in Europa besucht. Malerei studierte sie in Peking bei dem neorealistischen Maler Liu Xiaodong. In ihrer Interpretation des Mediums spiegelt sich die Auseinandersetzung mit asiatischer und westlicher Kunstgeschichte zweifellos wider – besonders mit jener Ölmalerei in der westlich beeinflussten Yōga-Tradition, die in der frühen Moderne in Japan entstand und nach dem Zweiten Weltkrieg zunächst urplötzlich verschwand, um bald abgelöst zu werden von Bewegungen wie Mona-ha oder Gutai. Das Porträt ist die Gattung, zu der Egami immer wieder zurückkehrt in der ihr eigenen Weise, indem sie, wie sie erläutert, „die Sensibilität asiatischer Menschen und ihre Auffassung von Perfektion [darstellt], aber mit westlichen Mitteln".

Aus diesem Zusammenspiel ergibt sich ihr Blick auf die Welt und auf den Menschen. „Ich benutze das Porträt, um die menschliche Natur, die menschlichen Instinkte, das Erkennen und die Fehlkommunikation zu entdecken", sagt sie. Vergänglichkeit der Schönheit wie des menschlichen Lebens kommen in ihren Bildern zum Ausdruck: „Es ist schwer zu erklären – ich liebe die Kirschblütentage. Die Blumen sind sehr schön, aber sie verschwinden plötzlich, nach einer Woche oder fünf Tagen. Ich denke über diese Dinge nach, wenn ich die menschlichen Porträts male."

Nur für einen flüchtigen Moment sichtbar und überwältigend – ebenfalls bloß aus der Distanz – ist auch das meteorologische Phänomen des Regenbogens. „Rainbow" hat Egami ihre Ausstellung im Rahmen des Mythenstein Projects genannt. Vom Regenbogen hat sich die Künstlerin für ihre Malerei die Farben und die parallelen Linien geliehen. Mehr noch: Der Regenbogen in seiner rätselhaften Schönheit ist für sie ein Symbol des Traums und der sich inmitten all der Fallstricke und Grauzonen von Kommunikation

herausschälenden Hoffnung – eine Hoffnung auch auf die Anerkennung von Unterschieden zwischen Menschen, auf friedliche Koexistenz und Diversität.
Egamis Bilder sind bewusst vieldeutig. Die Künstlerin will keine bestimmte Rezeption vorgeben – im Gegenteil. Was man in den Werken sieht, hängt stark von dem Individuum ab, das ihnen gegenübersteht. Die eine Wahrheit, die eine Bedeutung existiert nicht, sie findet und erfindet sich immer neu, da ist Egami ganz bei Derrida.

12   RAINBOW – Between Sound Wave and Light Wave, 2024
Oil on canvas / Öl auf Leinwand
77 ½ × 50 ⅜ in. / 197 × 128 cm

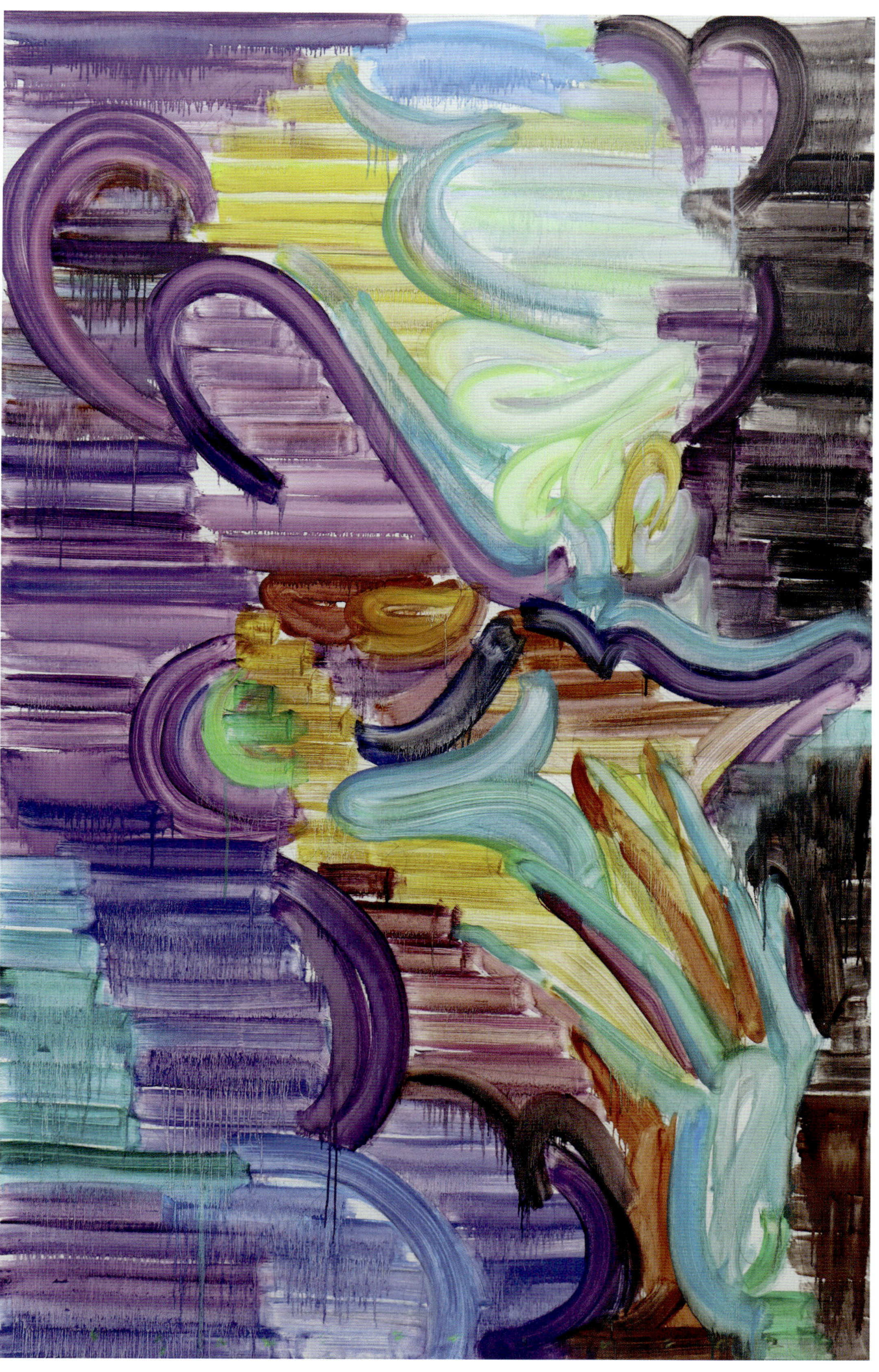

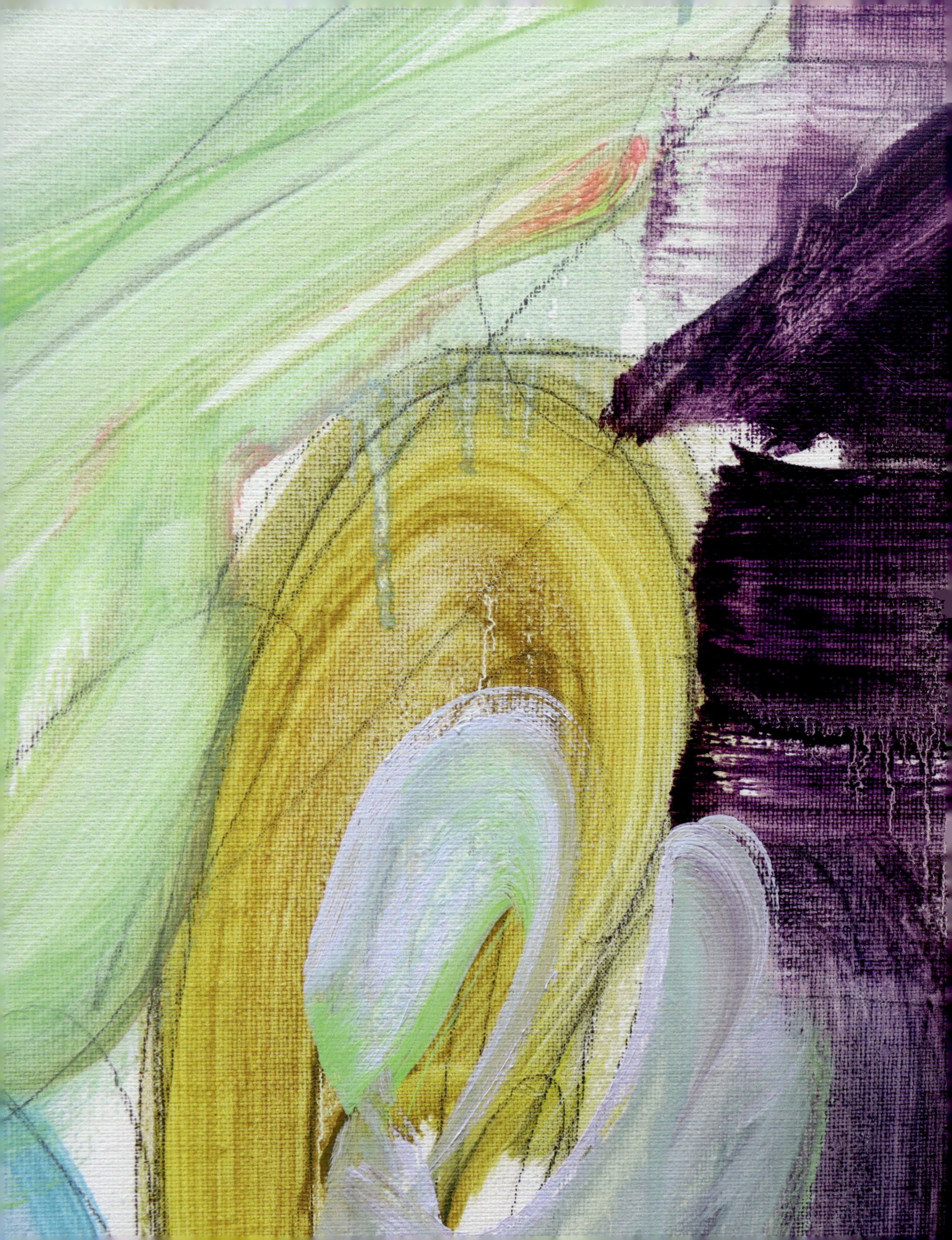

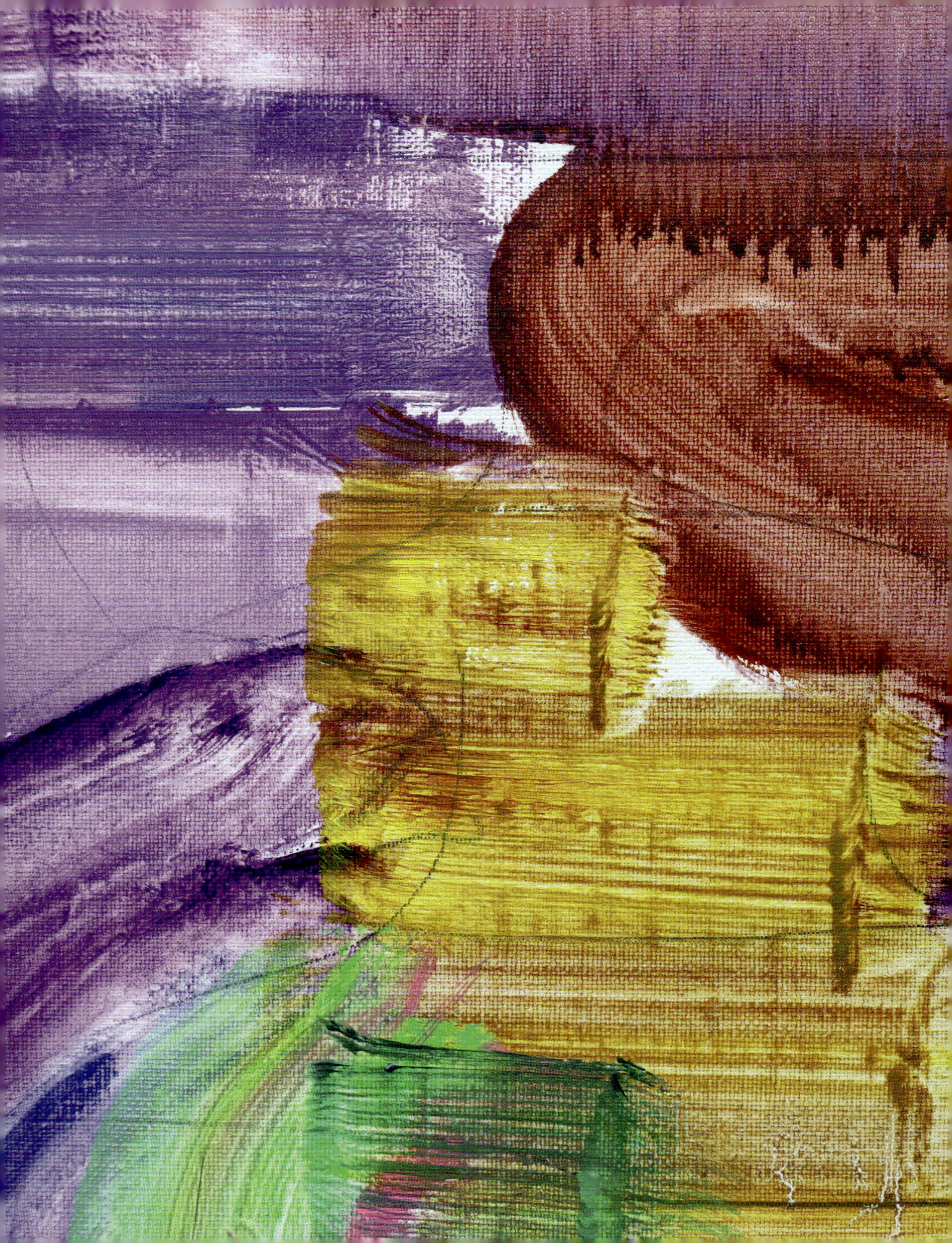

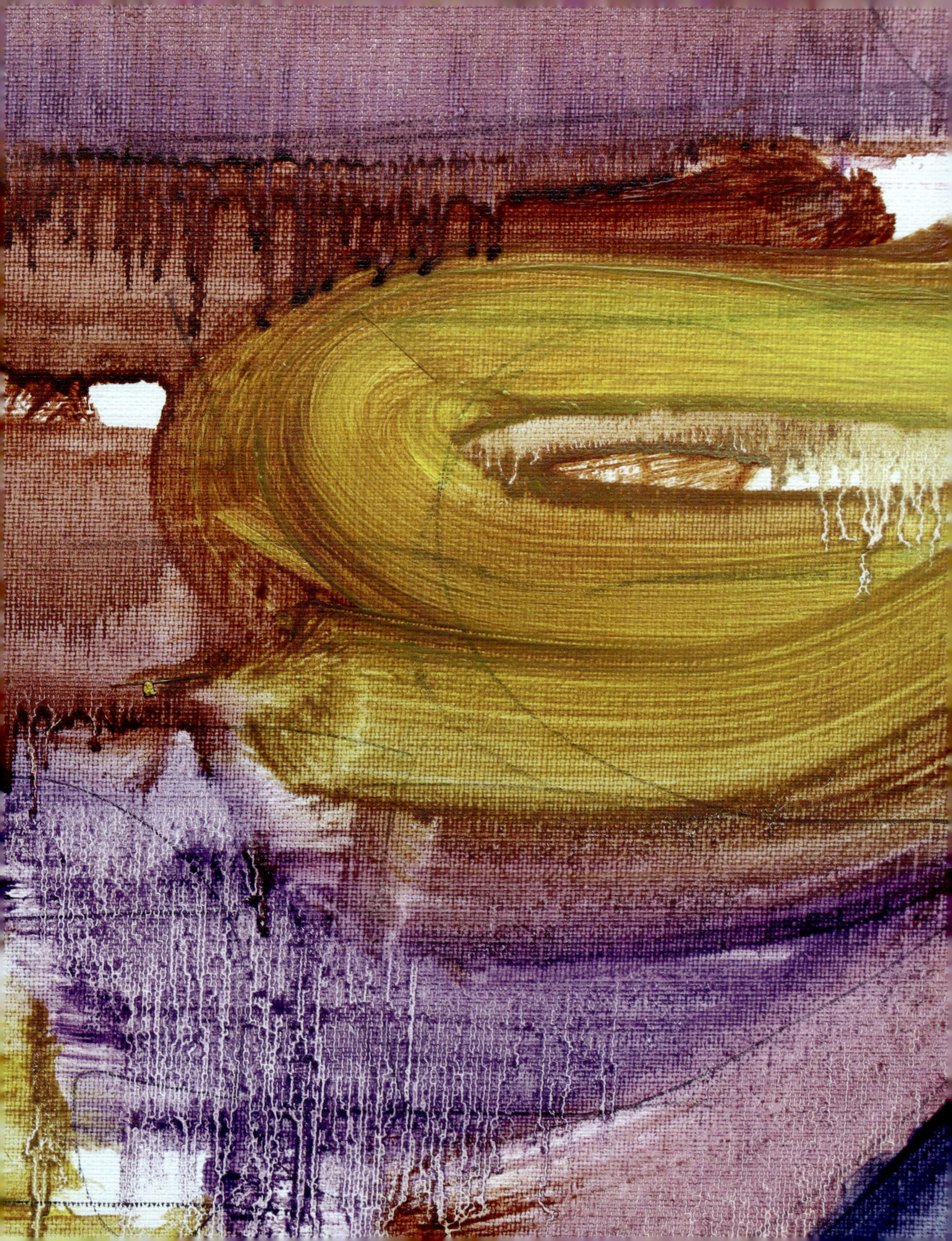

18   RAINBOW – Between Sound Wave and Light Wave, 2024
Oil on canvas / Öl auf Leinwand
77 ¾ × 50 ⅜ in. / 197,5 × 128 cm

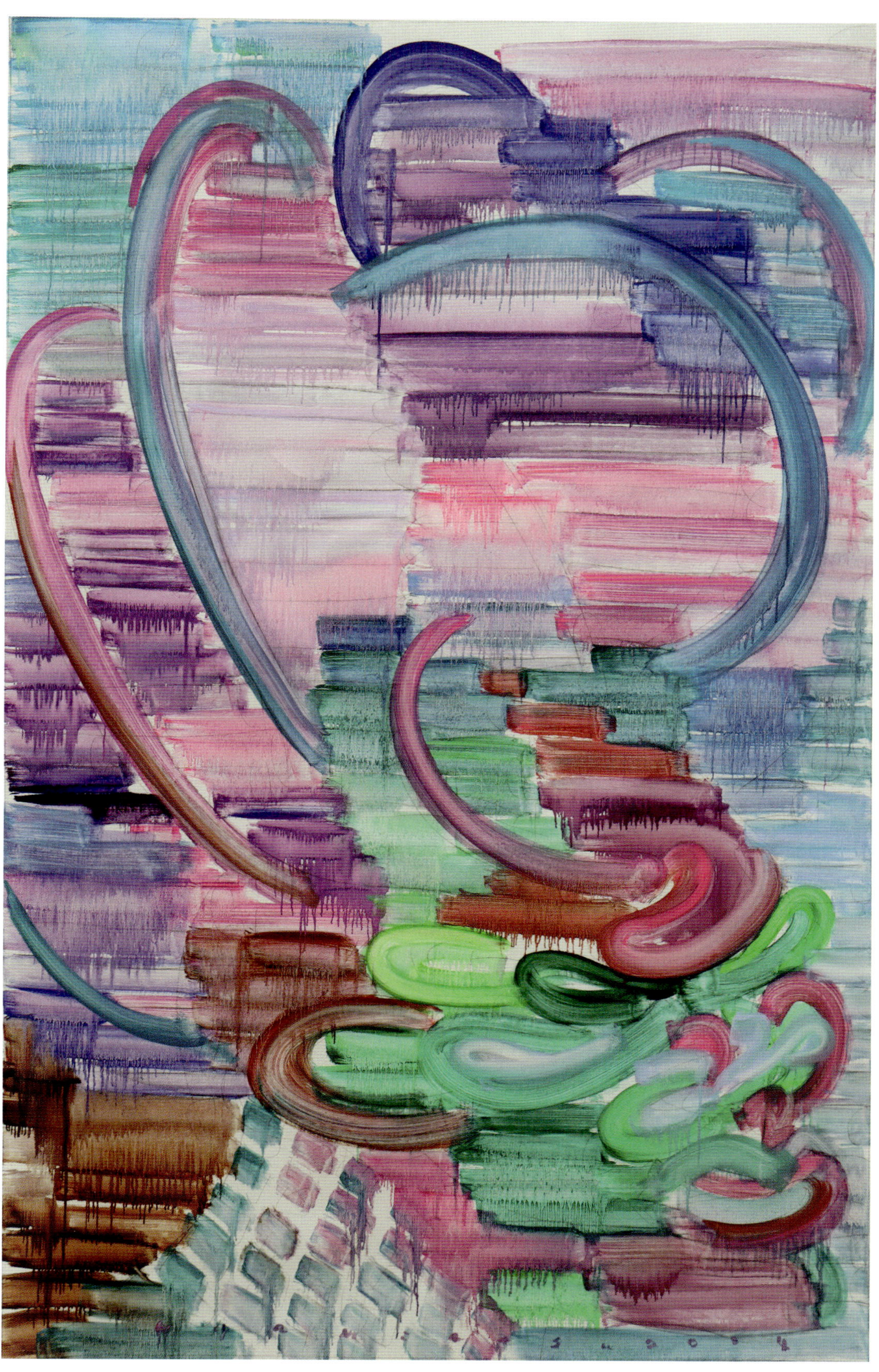

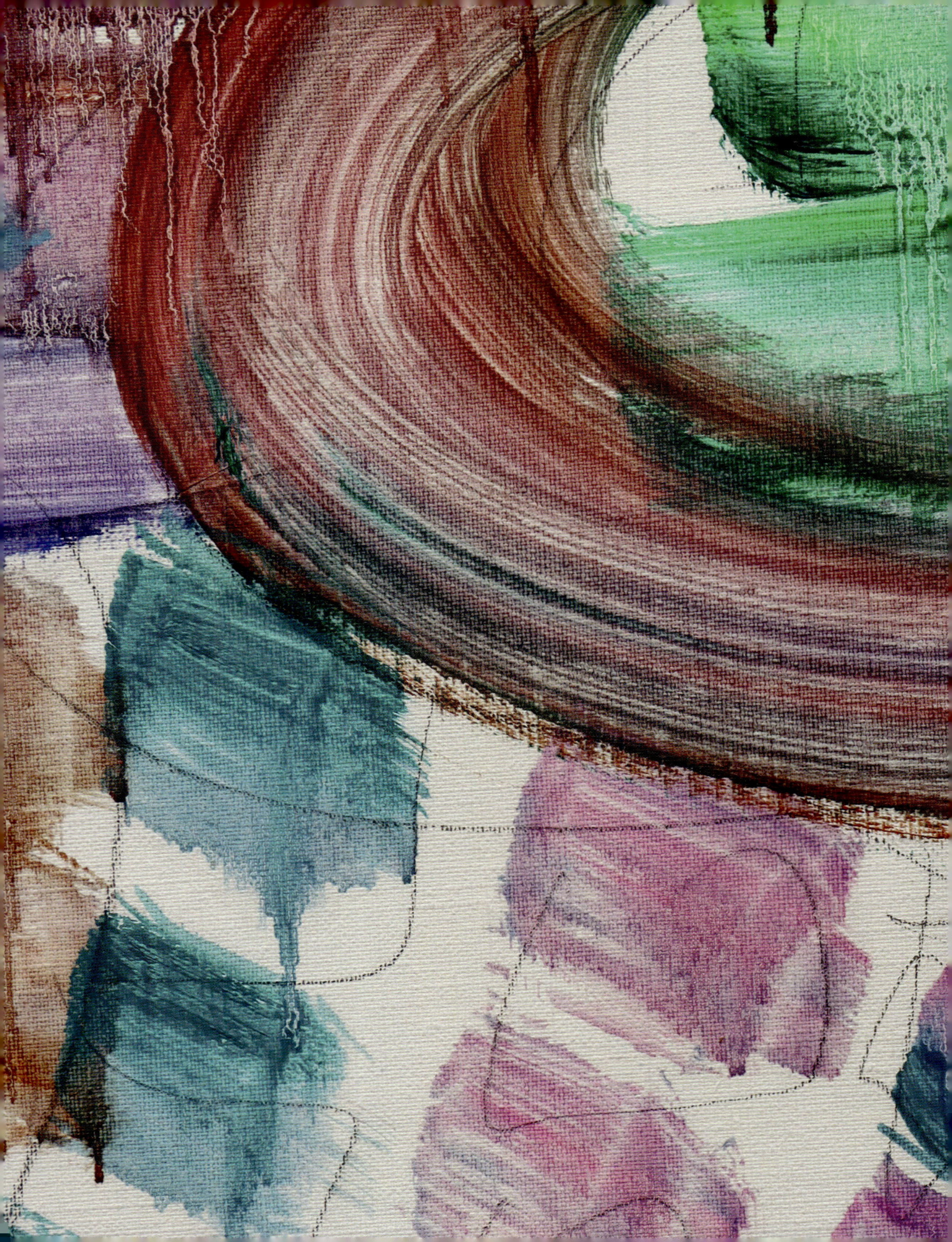

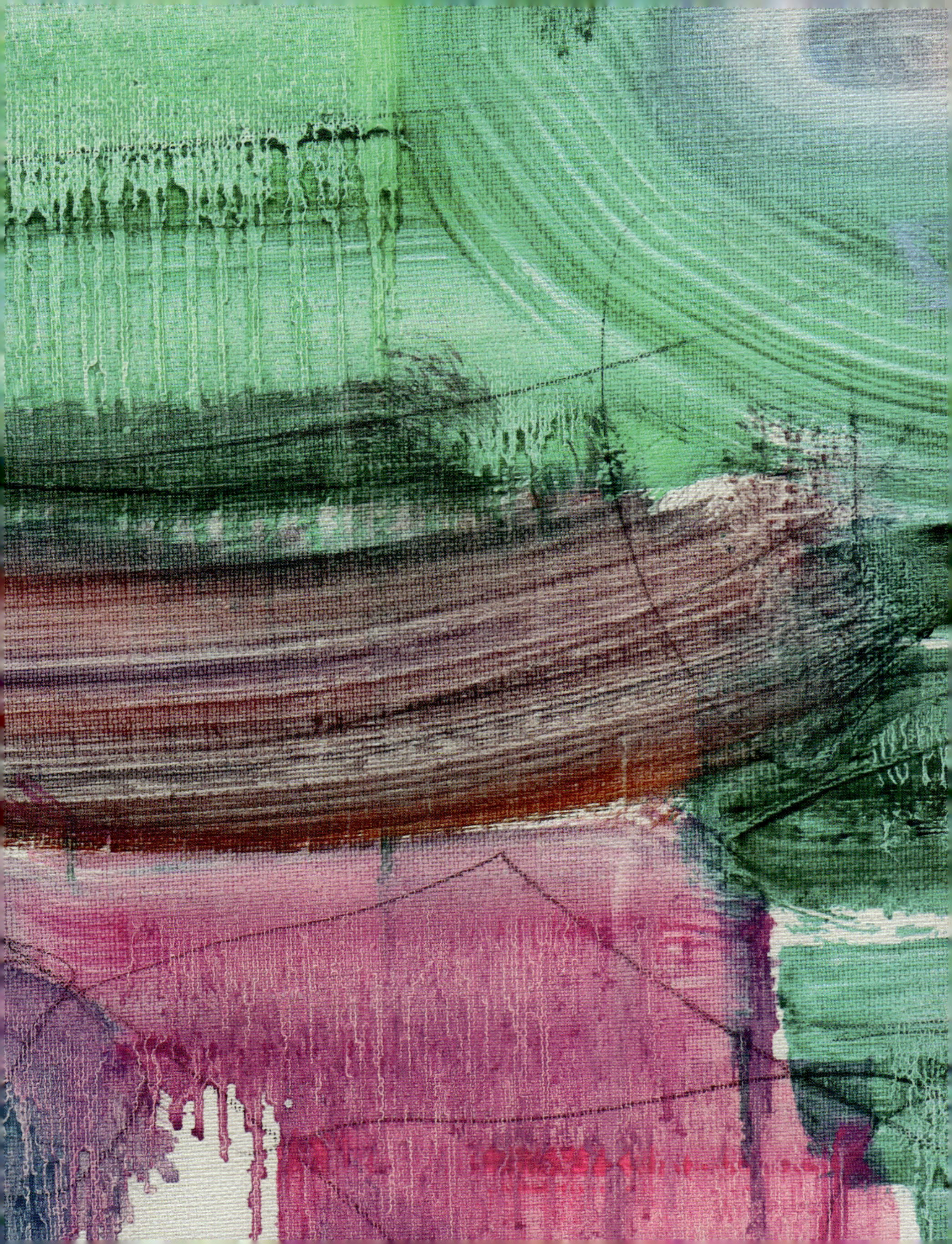

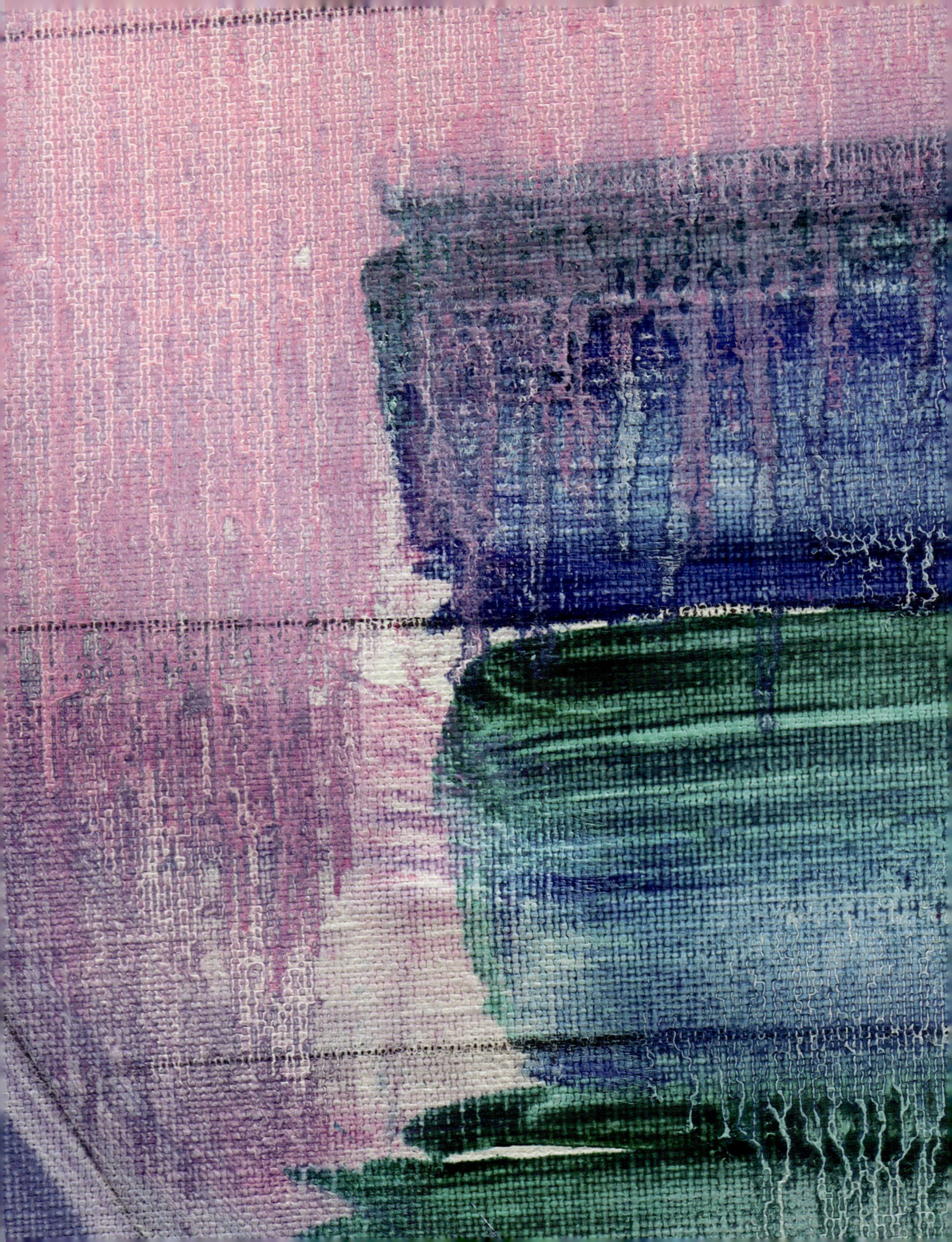

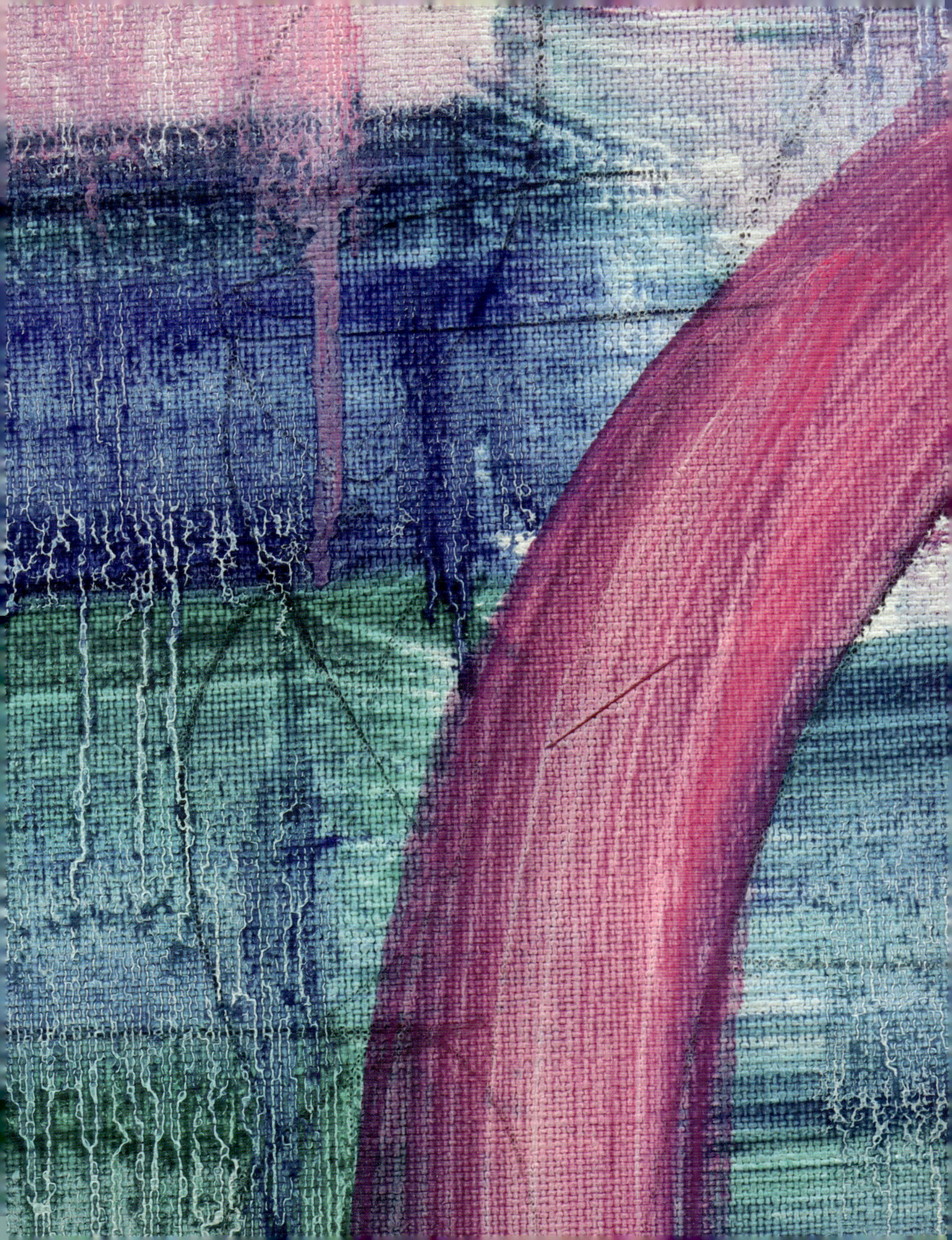

24   RAINBOW – Life Line, 2024
Oil on canvas / Öl auf Leinwand
78 ½ × 53 ¾ in. / 199,5 × 136,5 cm

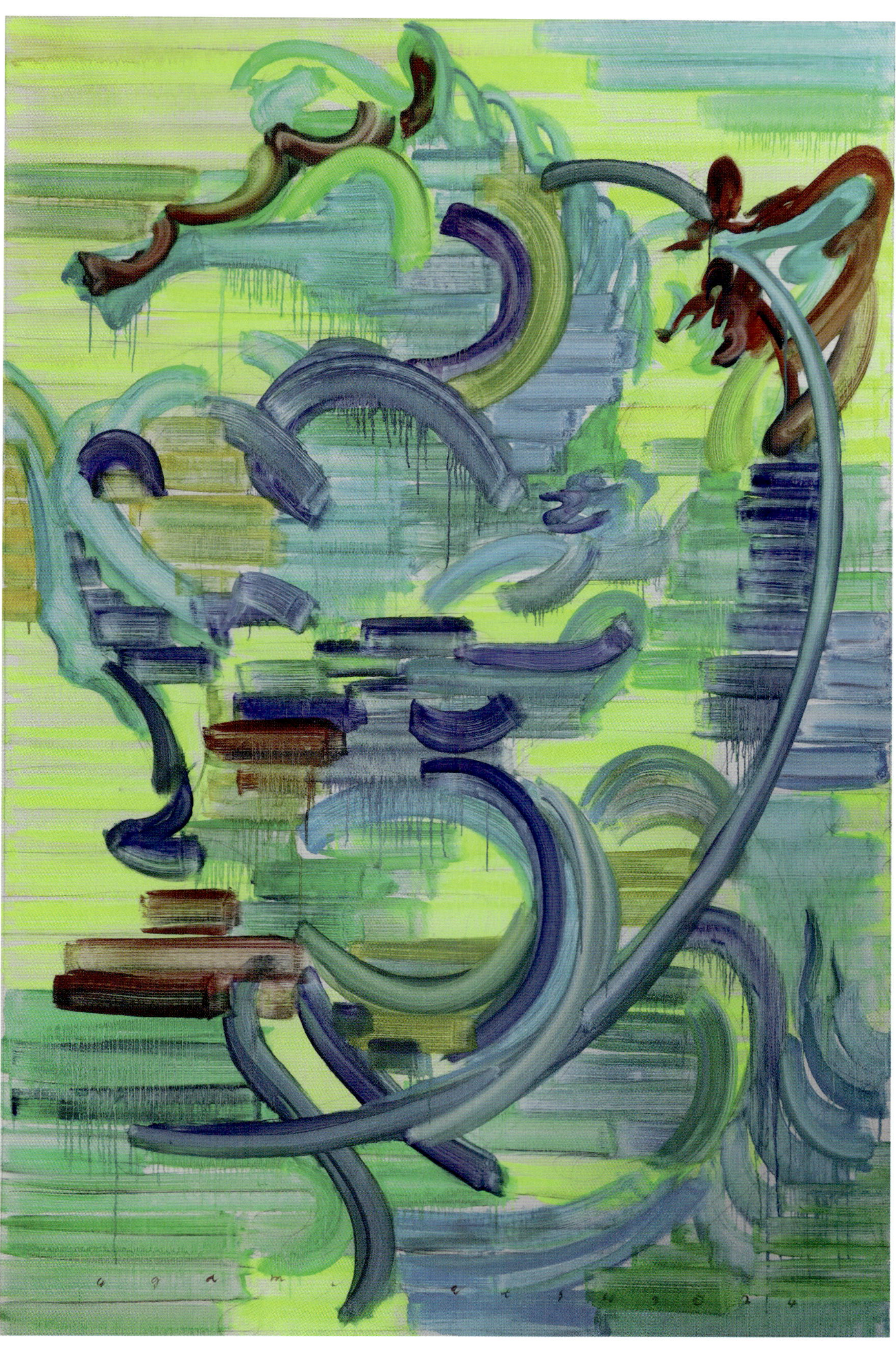

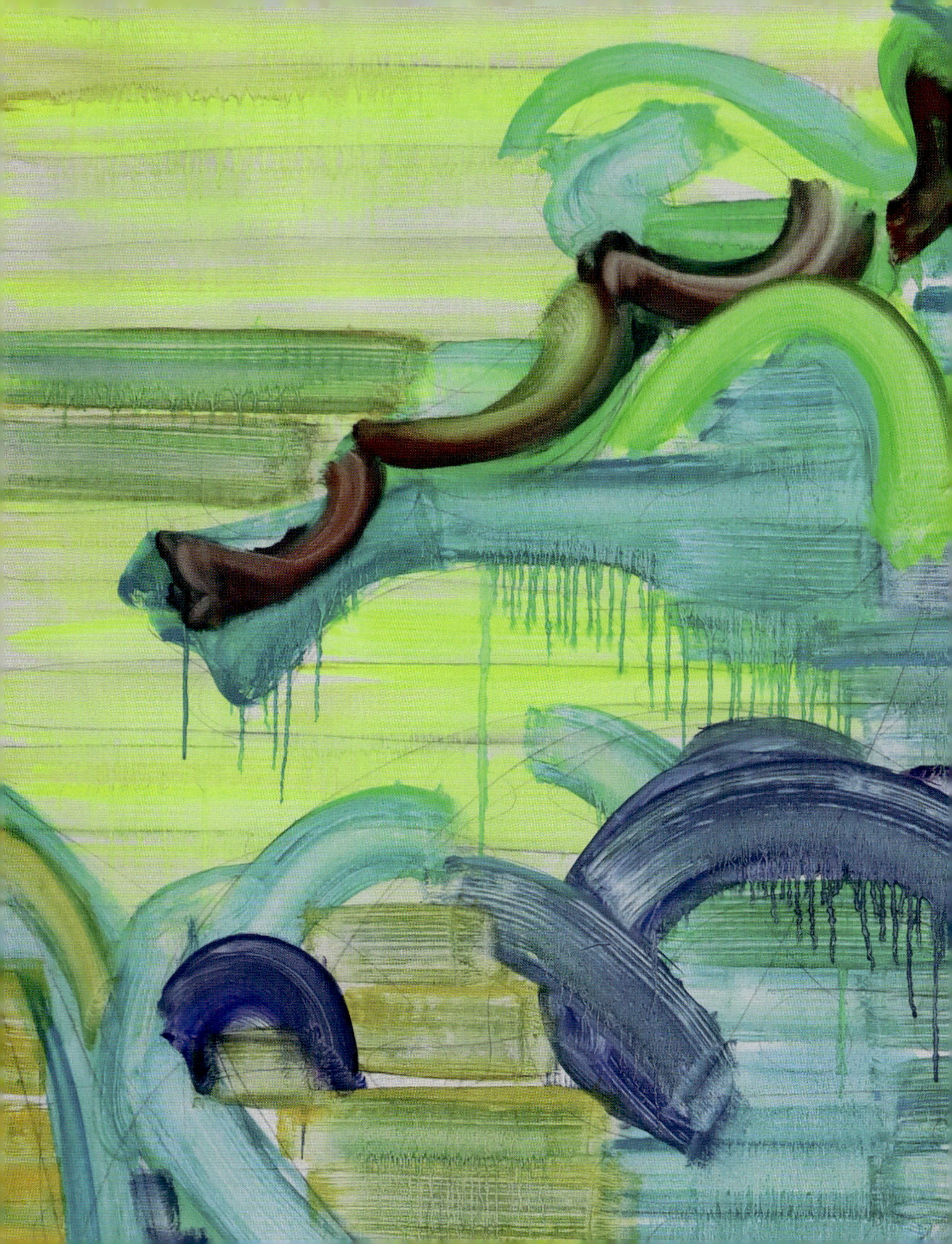

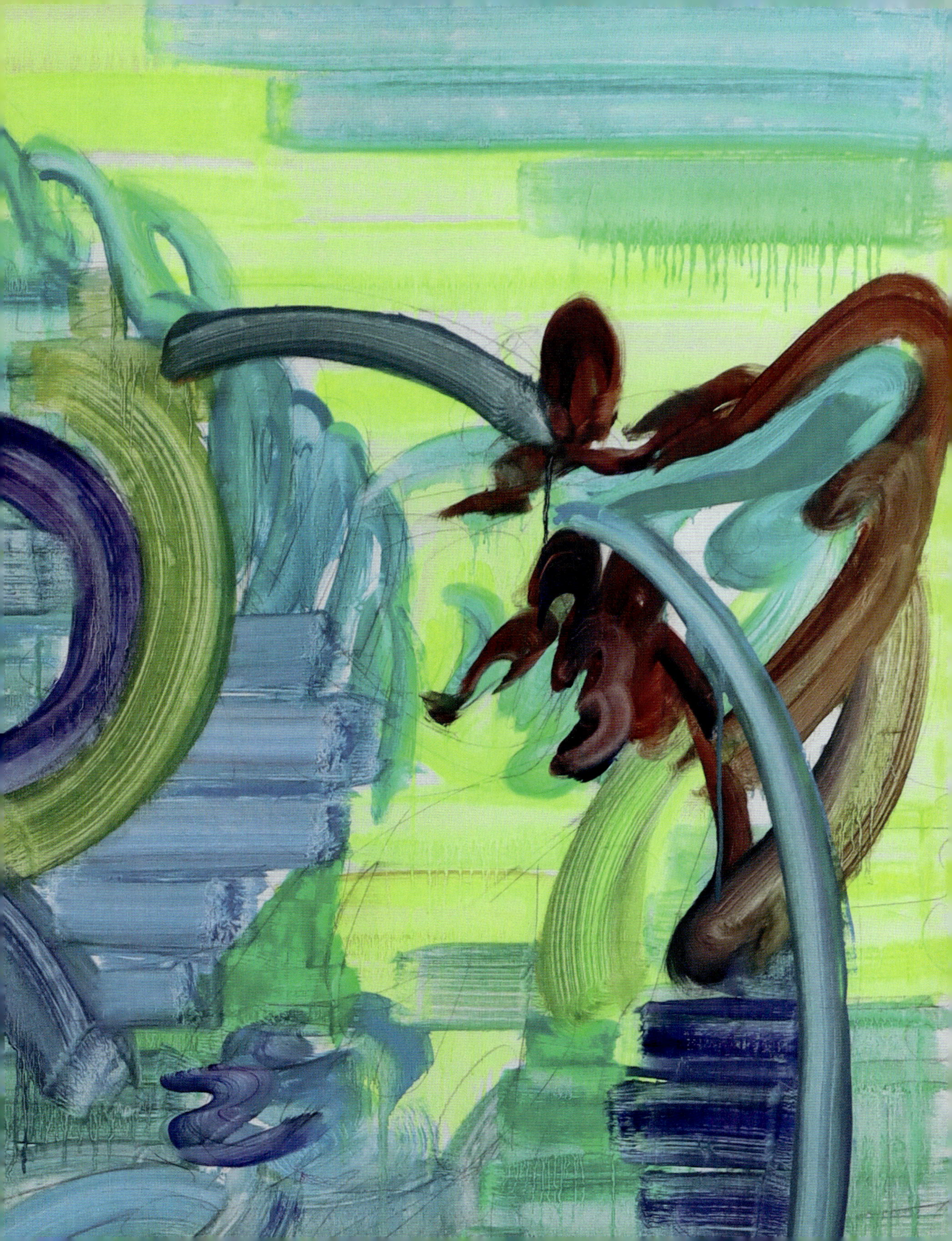

28   RAINBOW – Life Line, 2024
Oil on canvas / Öl auf Leinwand
78 ½ × 54 ⅜ in. / 199,5 × 138 cm

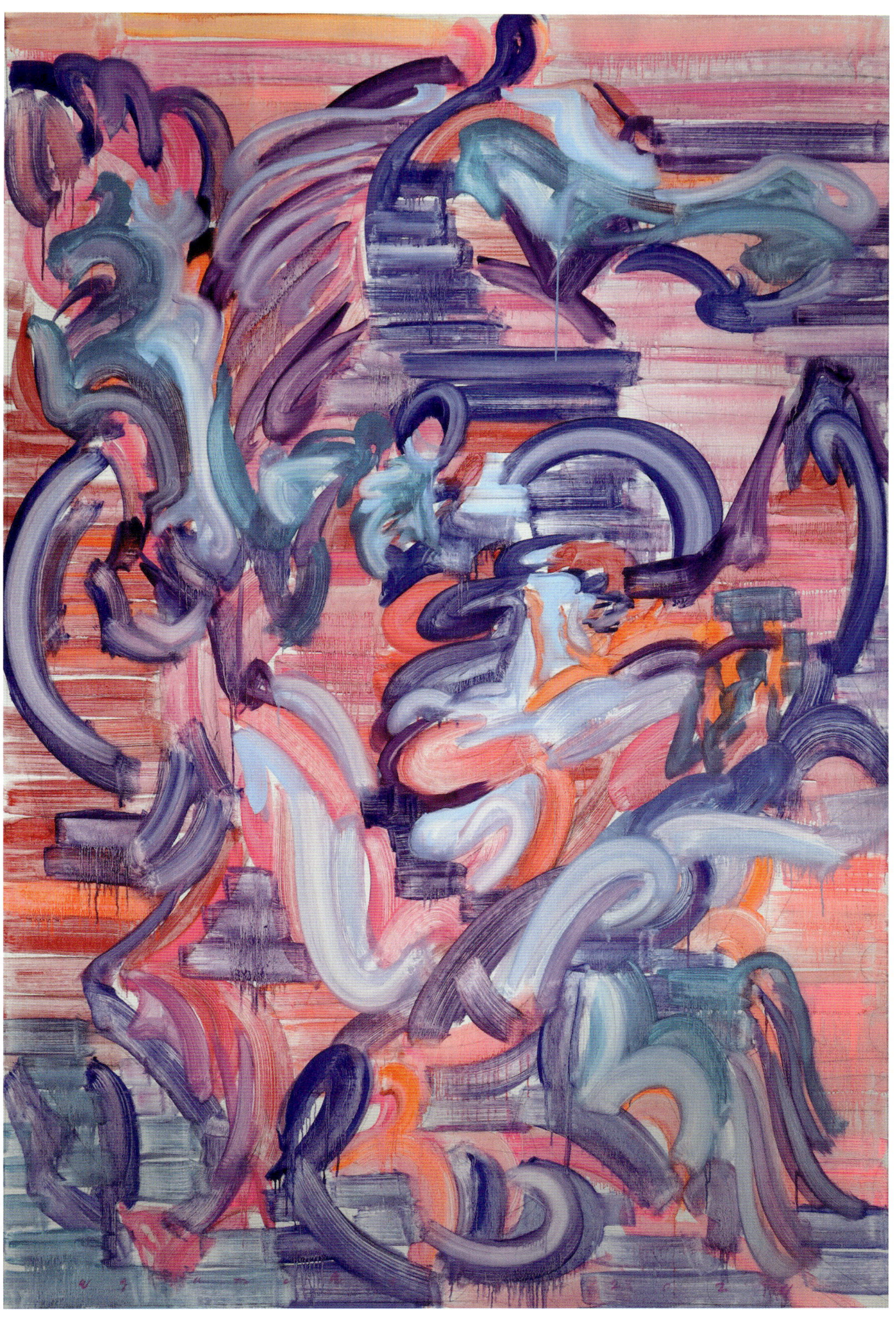

30 RAINBOW – 002, 2024
Oil on canvas / Öl auf Leinwand
36 × 54 ⅞ in. / 91,5 × 139,5 cm

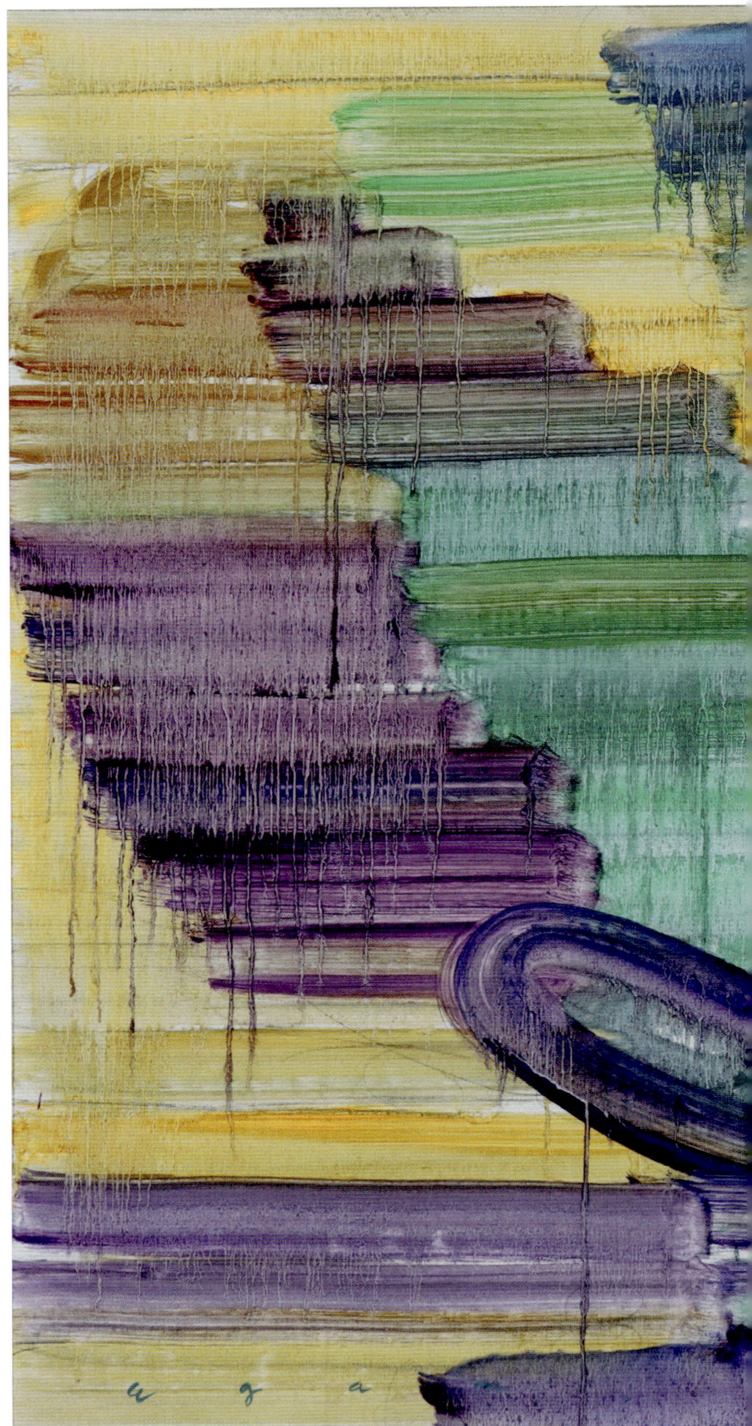

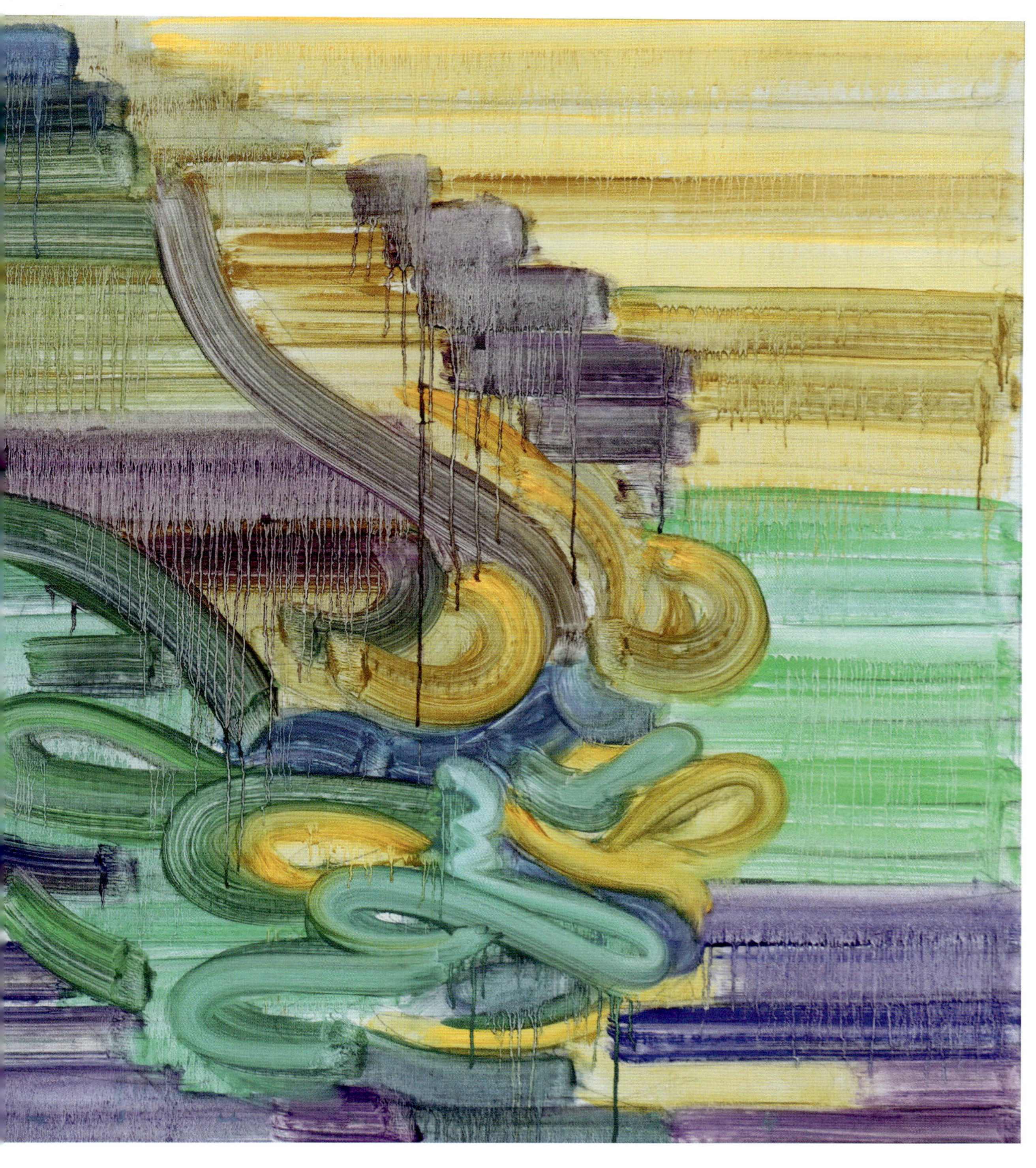

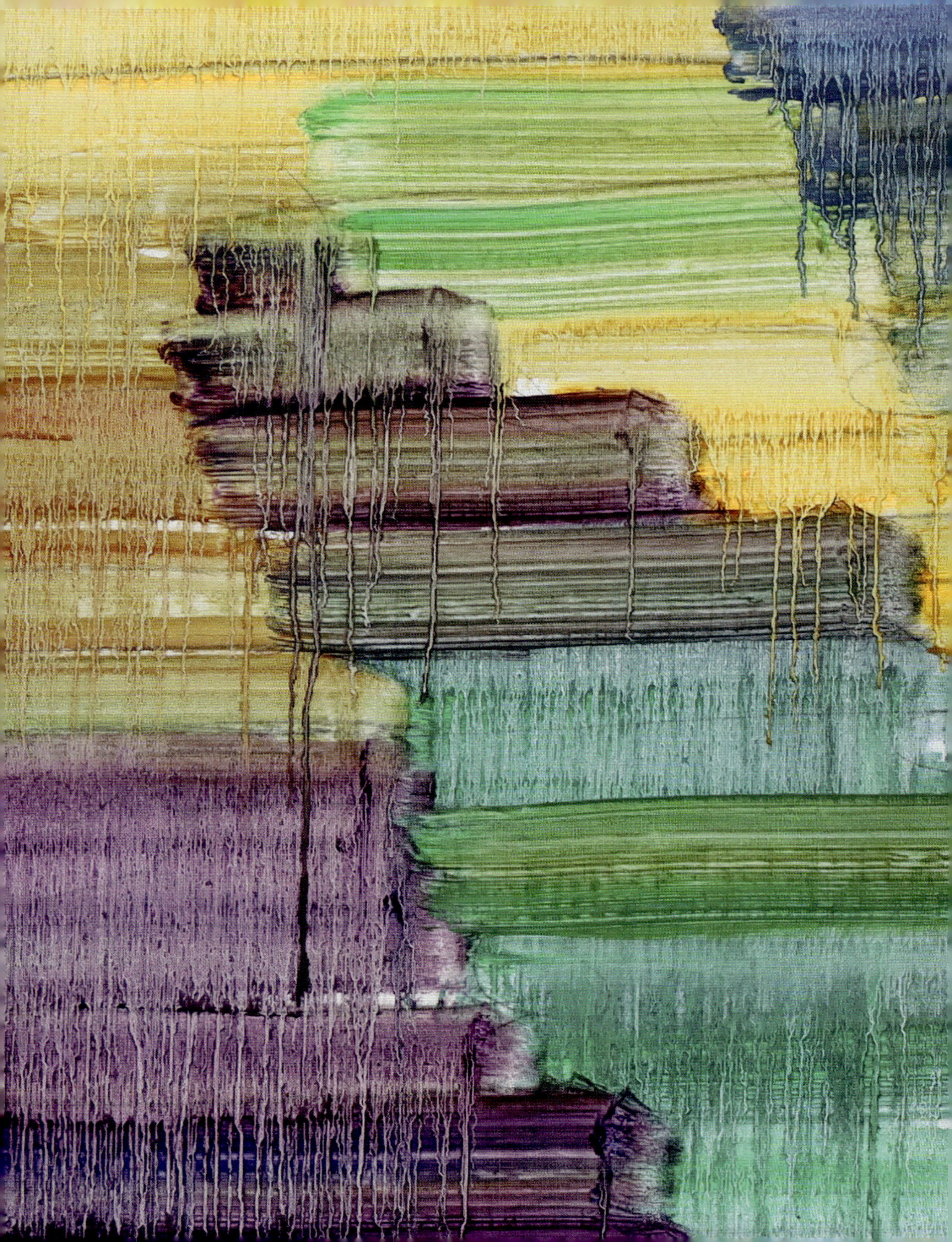

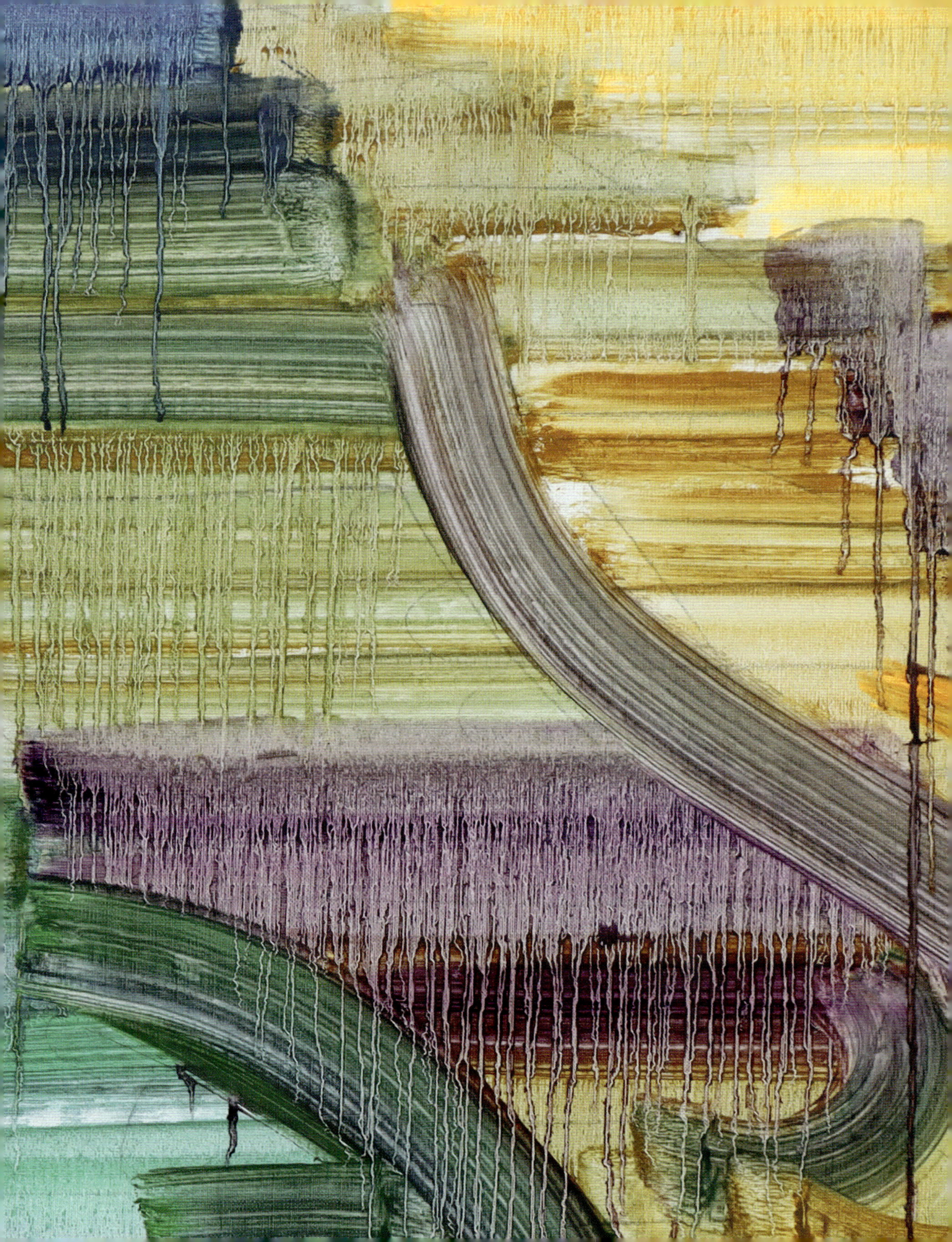

34   RAINBOW – 003, 2024
Oil on canvas / Öl auf Leinwand
36 × 54 ⅞ in. / 91,5 × 139,5 cm

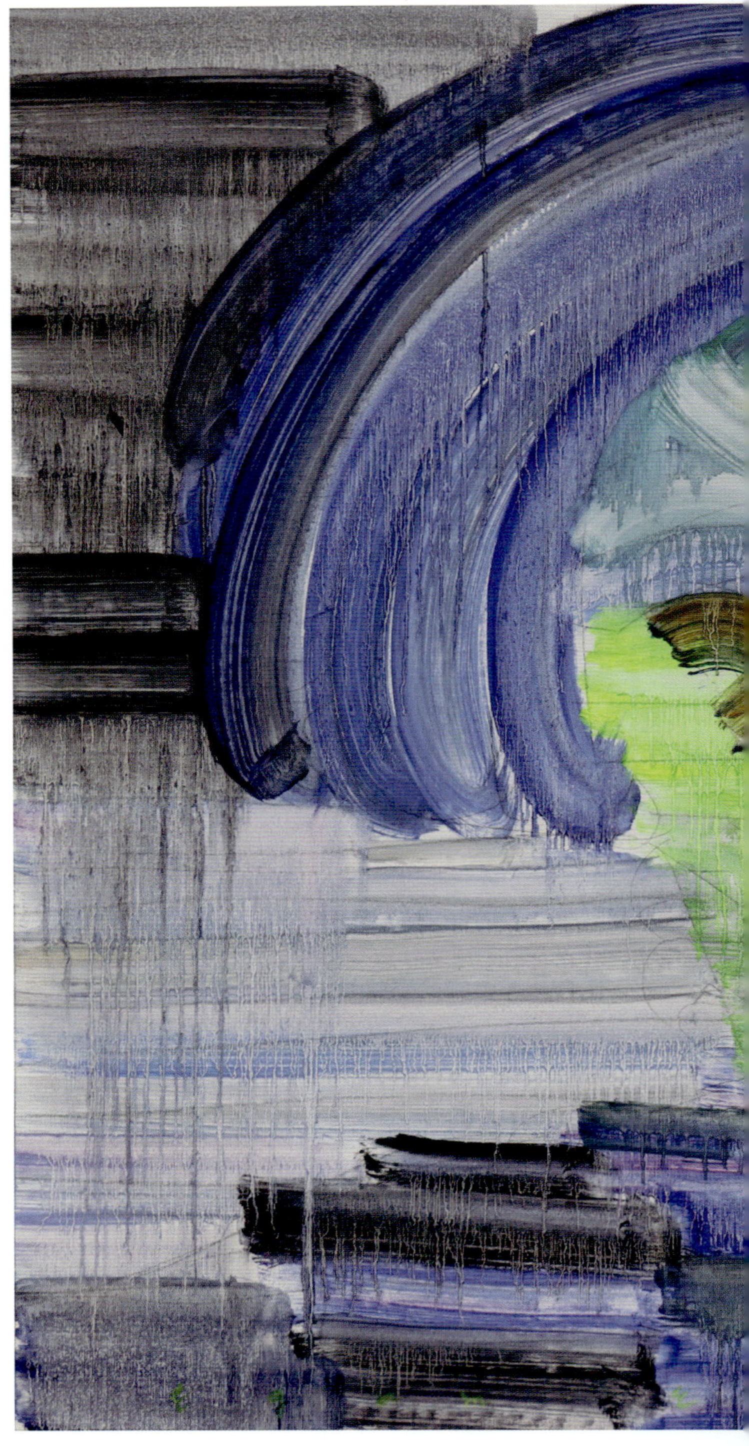

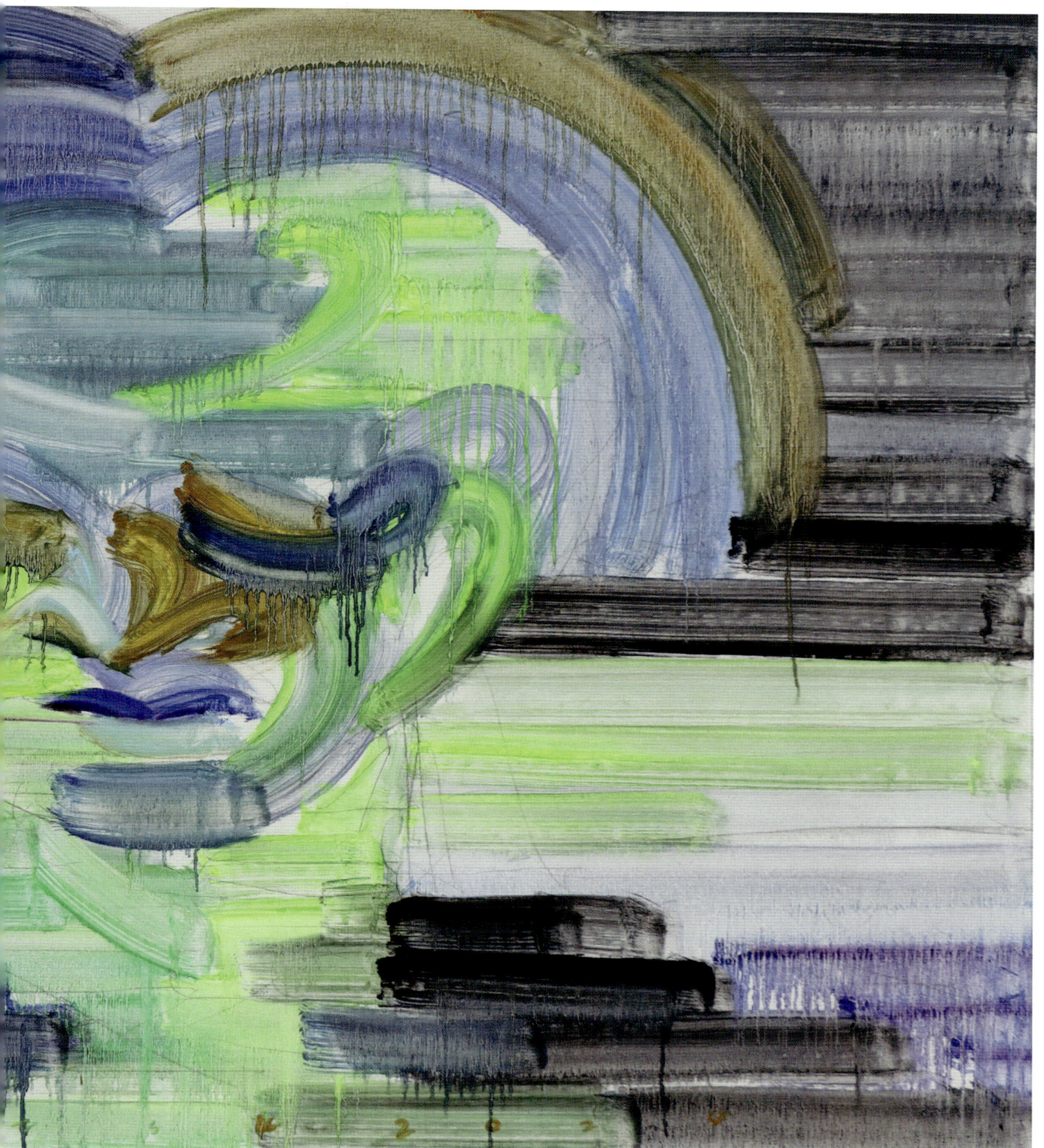

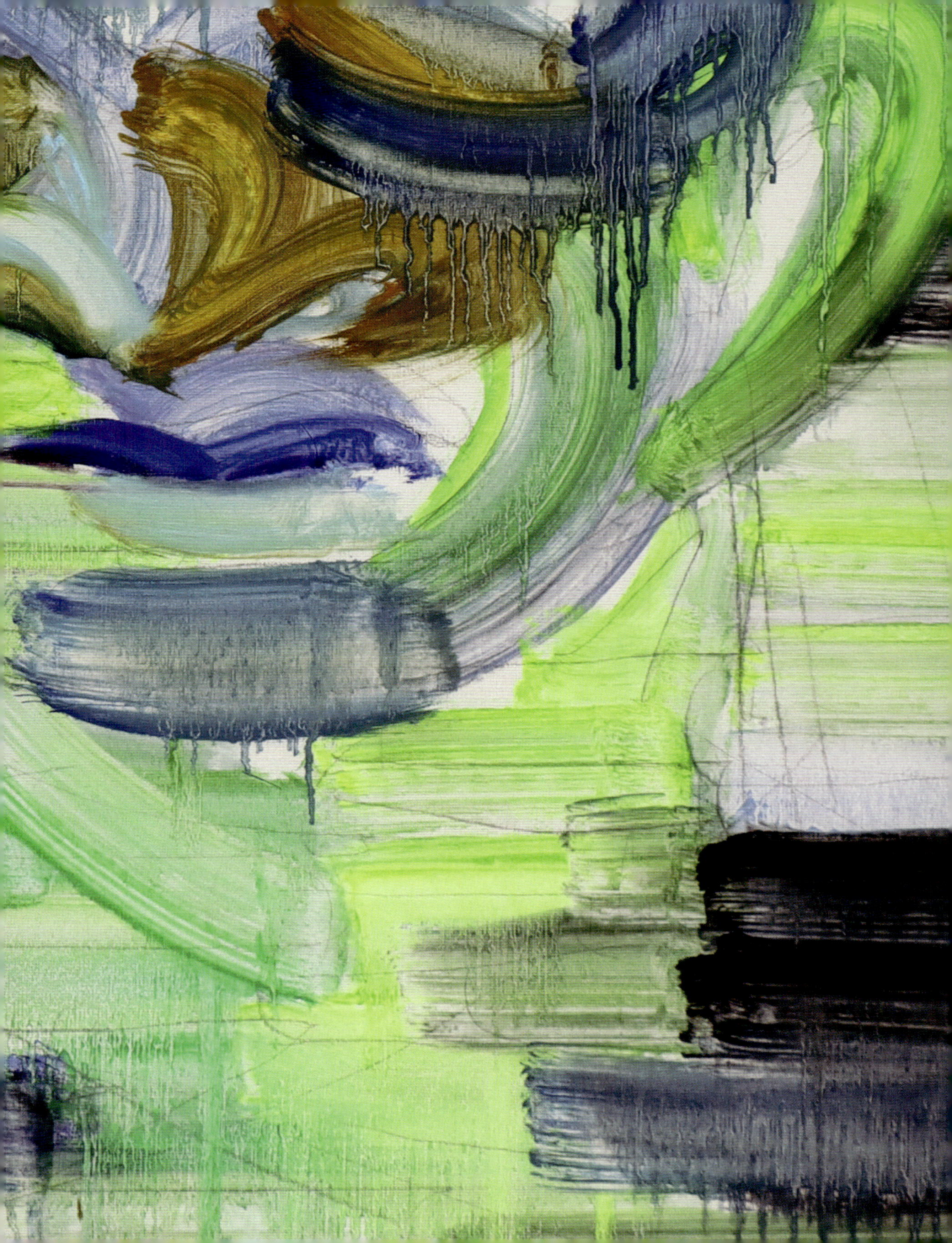

38   RAINBOW – 006, 2024
Oil on canvas / Öl auf Leinwand
31 1/8 × 23 3/8 in. / 79 × 59,5 cm

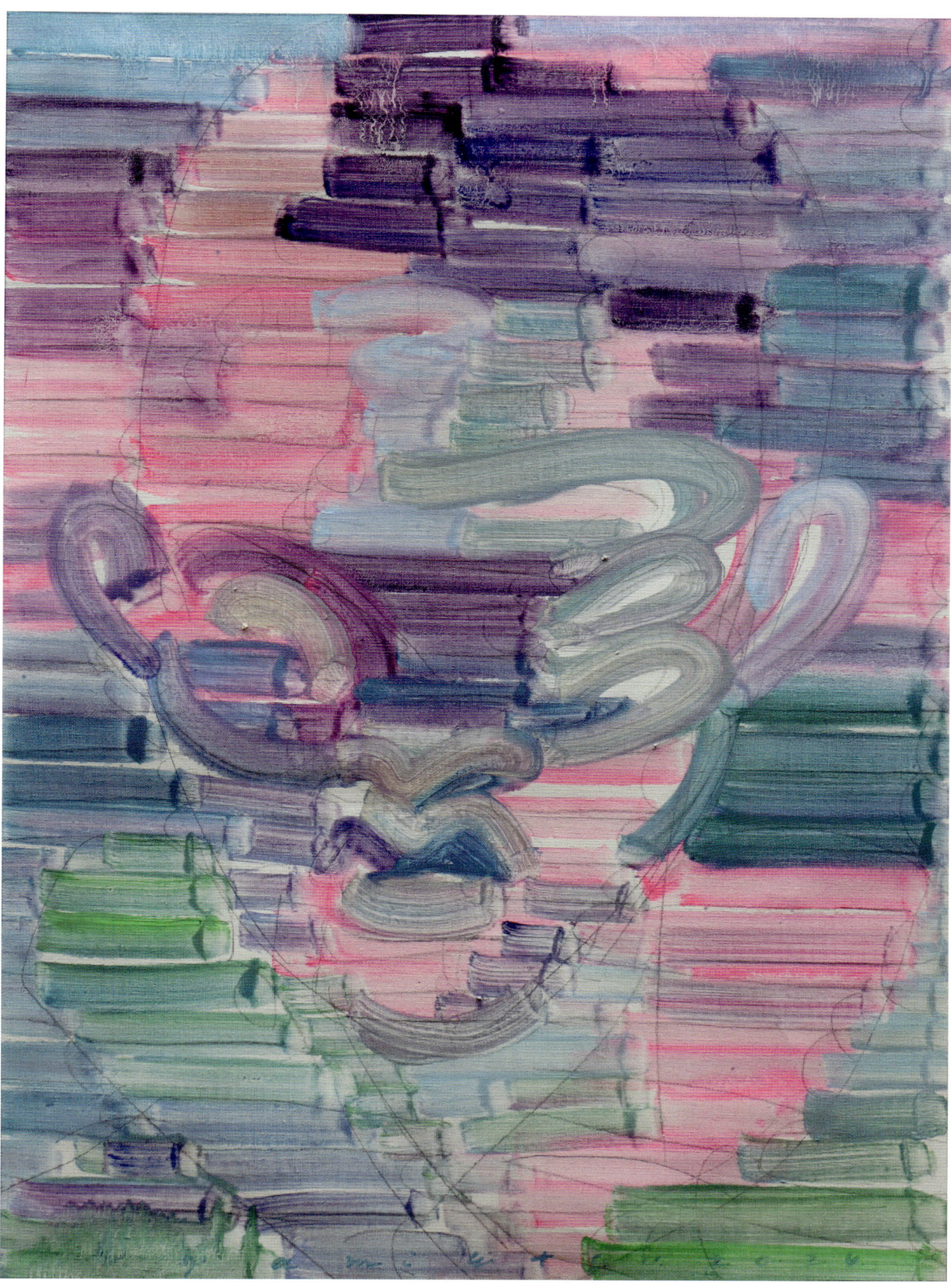

40   RAINBOW – 007, 2024
Oil on canvas / Öl auf Leinwand
30 ¾ × 23 ⅝ in. / 78 × 60 cm

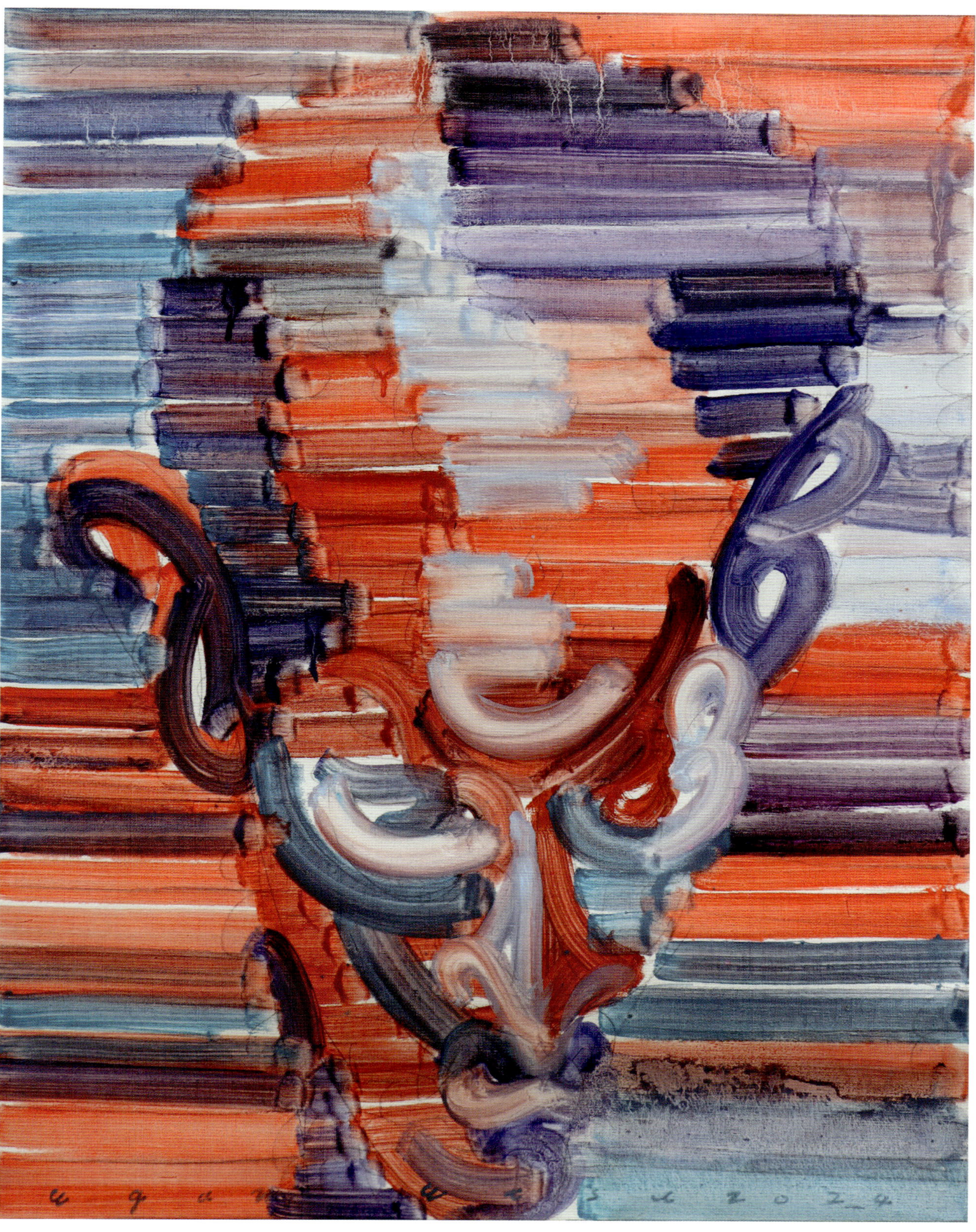

42   RAINBOW – 008, 2024
Oil on canvas / Öl auf Leinwand
31 ½ × 23 ⅝ in. / 80 × 60 cm

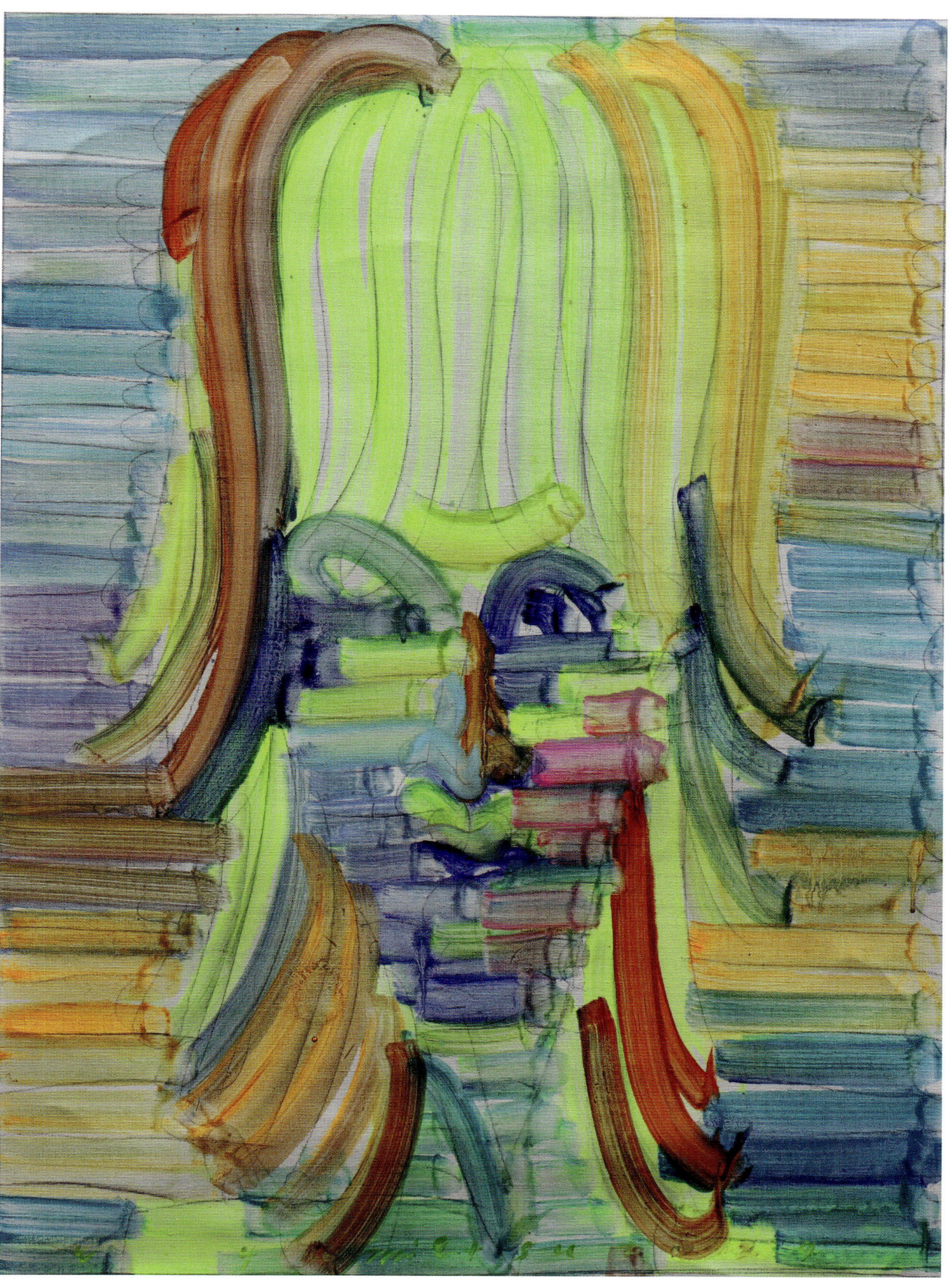

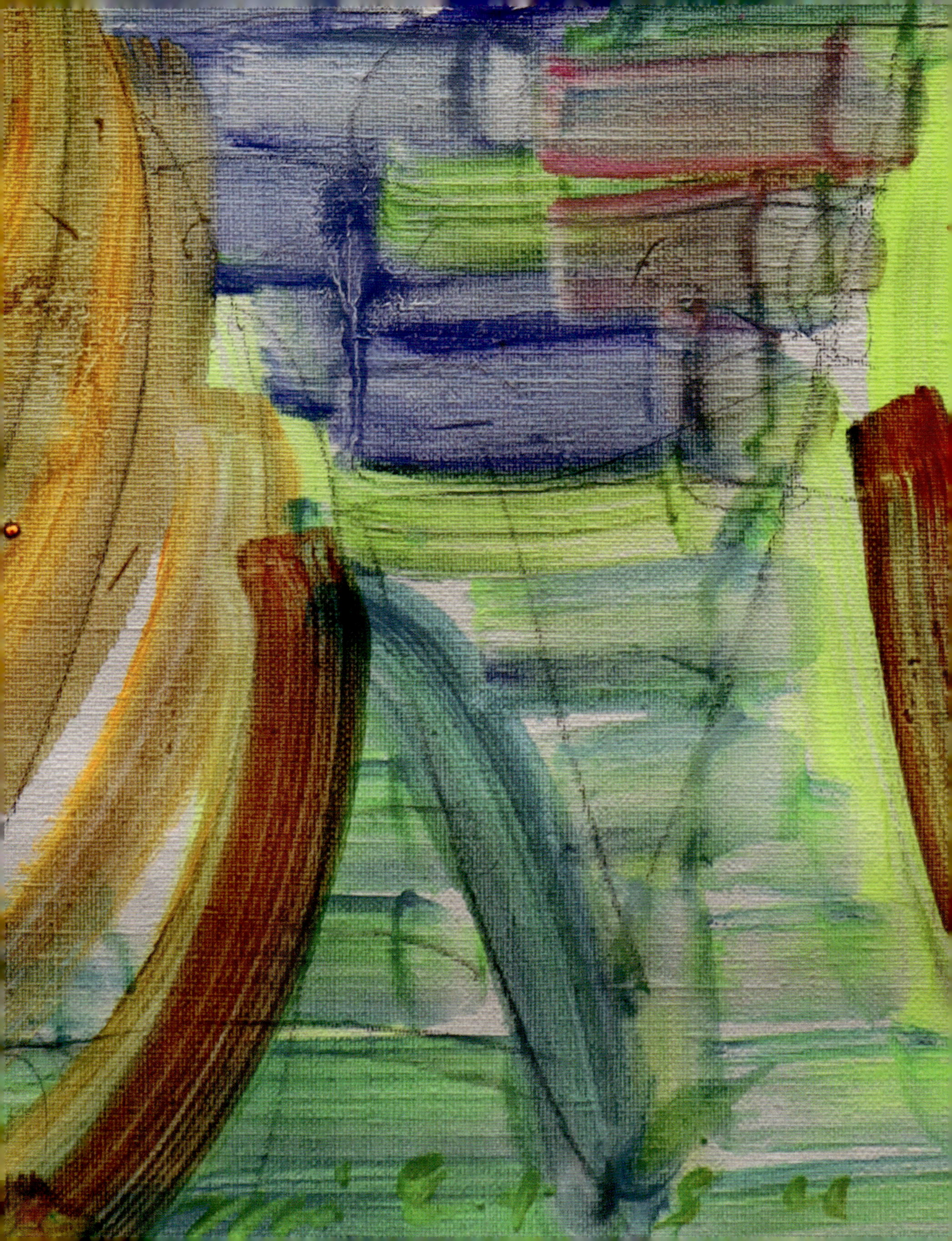

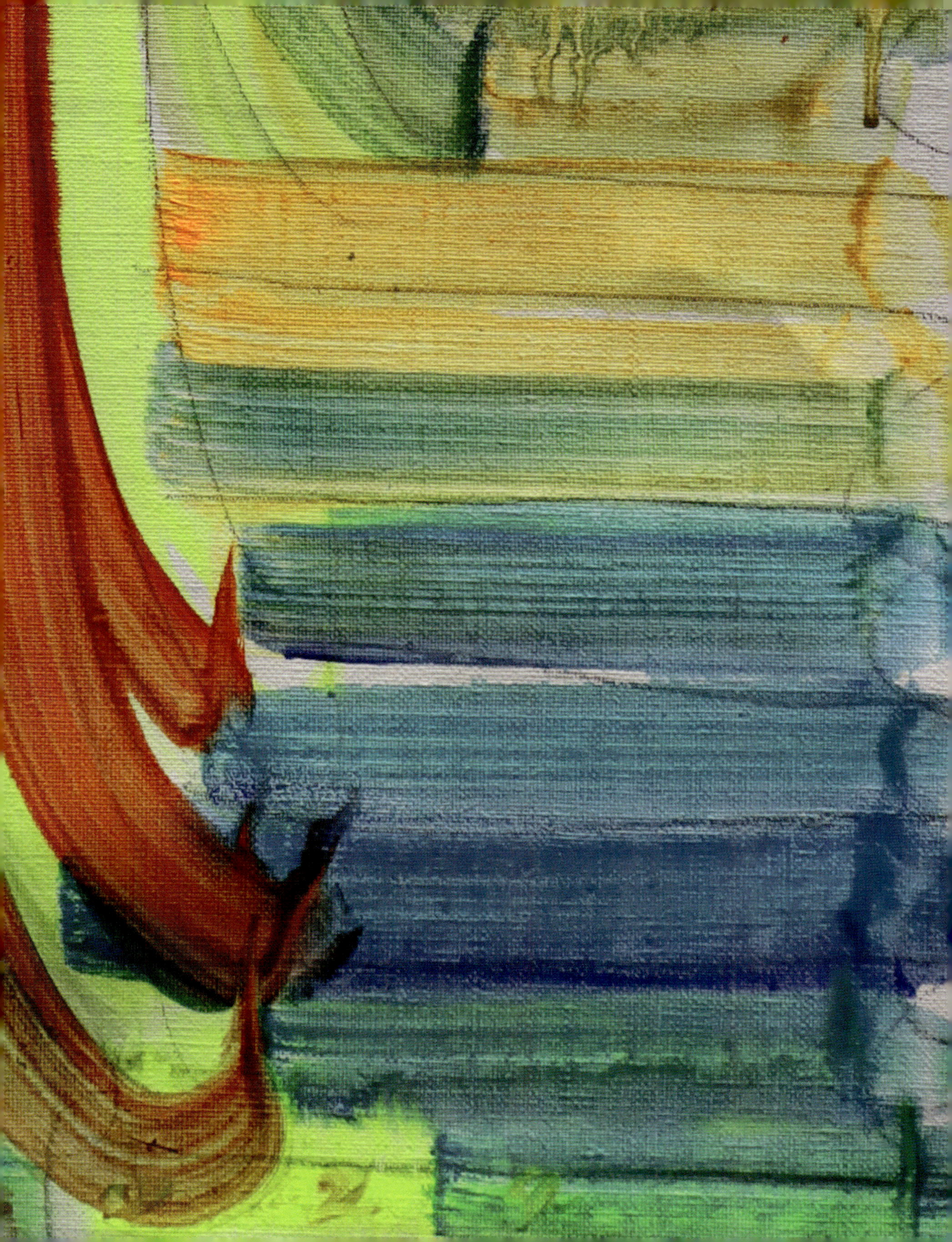

46   RAINBOW – 009, 2024
Oil on canvas / Öl auf Leinwand
16 ⅜ × 35 ¼ in. / 41,5 × 89,5 cm

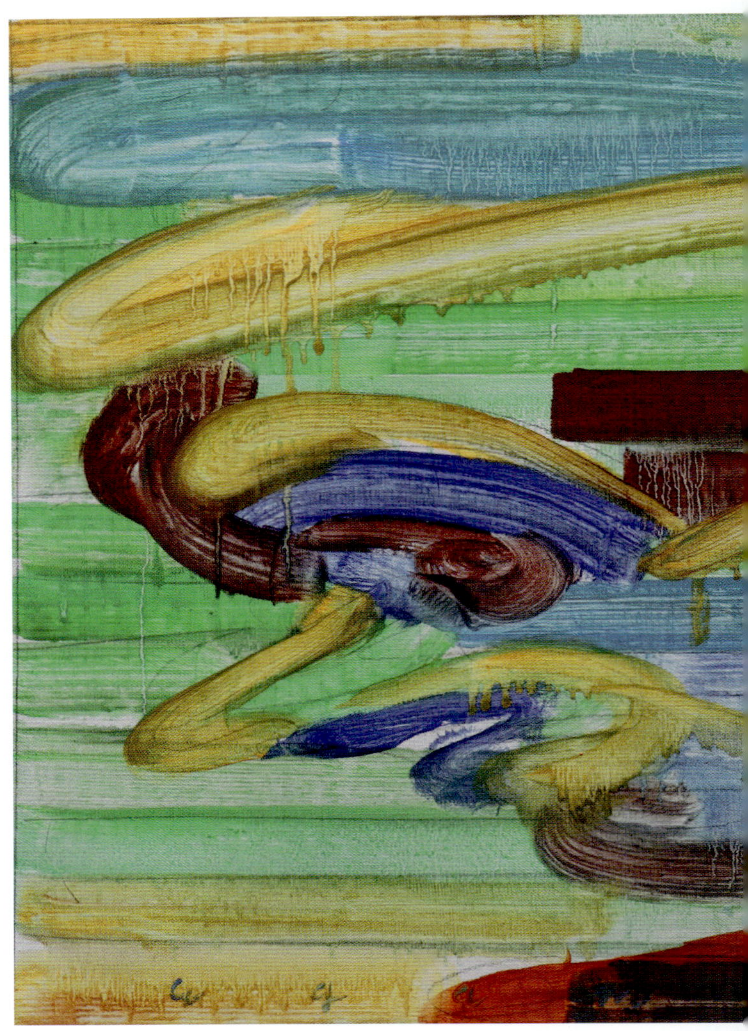

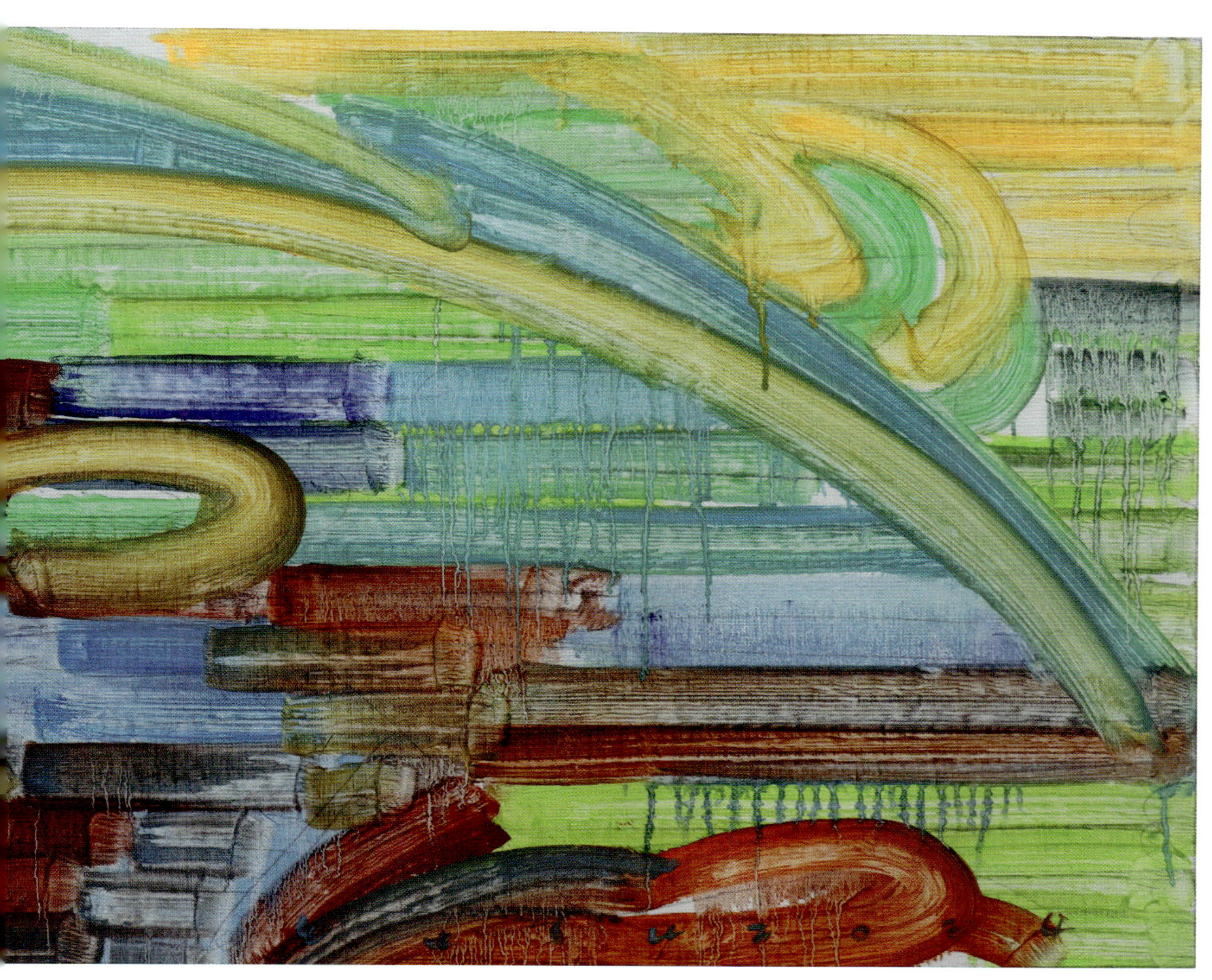

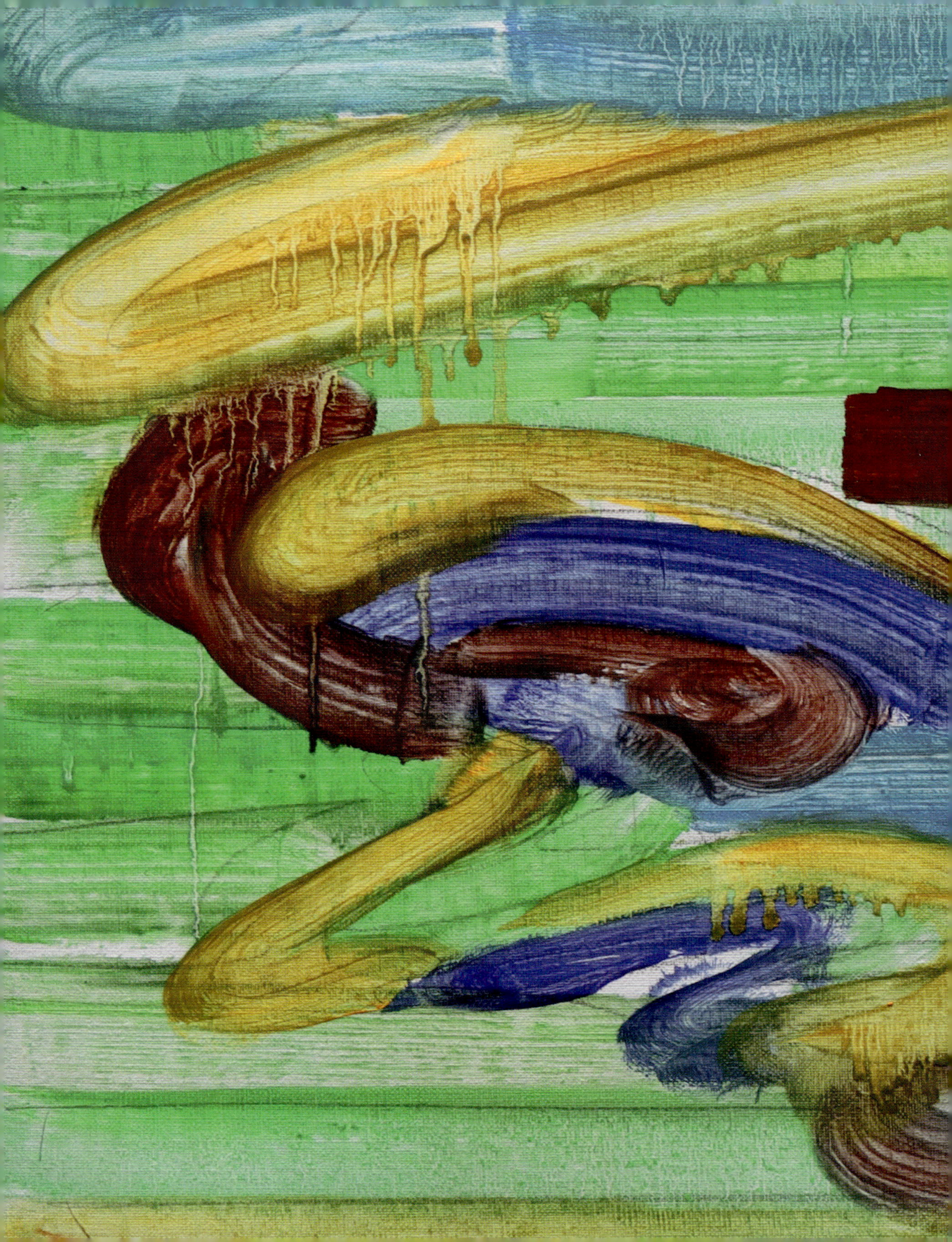

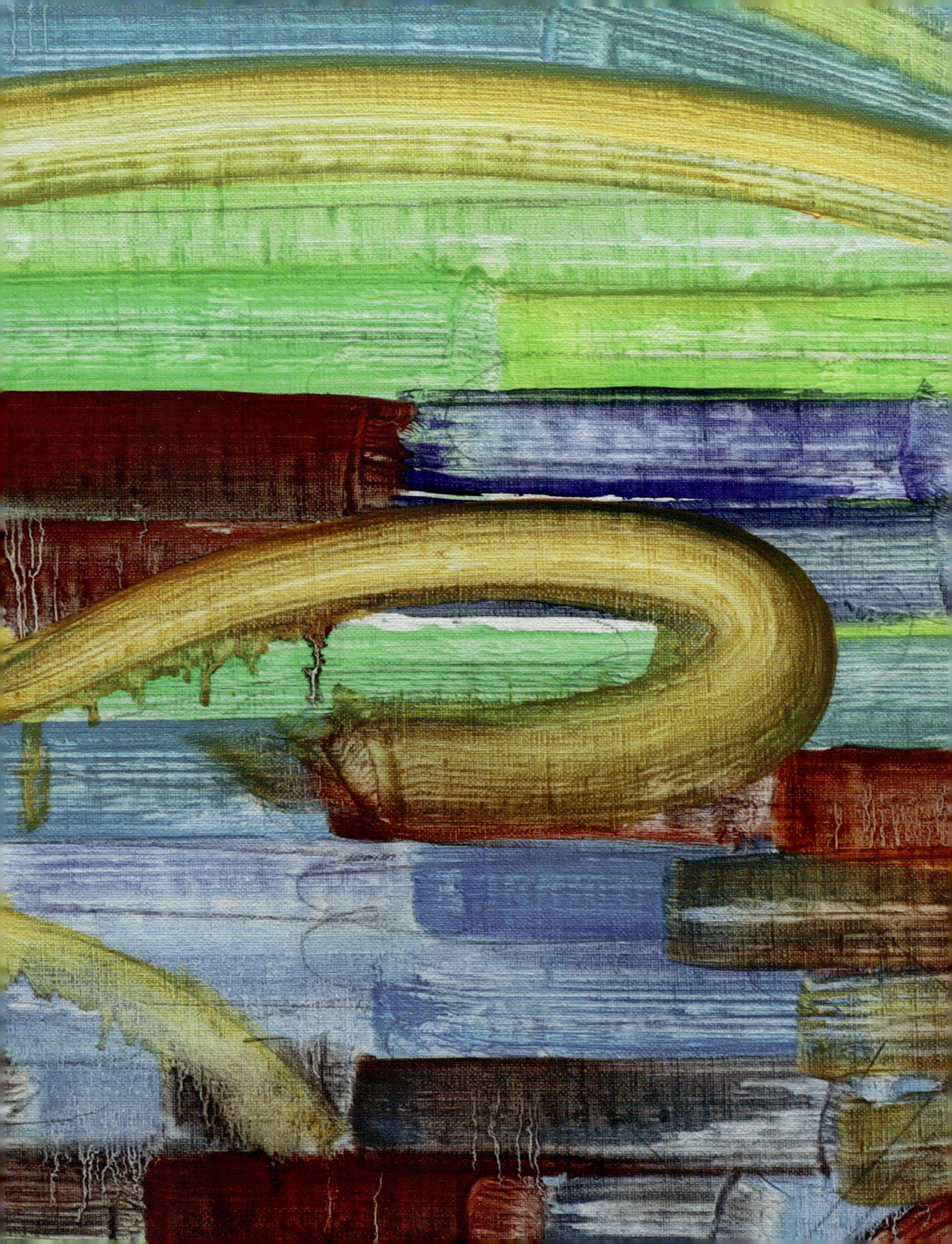

50   RAINBOW – 010, 2024
Oil on canvas / Öl auf Leinwand
27 × 19 ⅛ in. / 68,5 × 48,5 cm

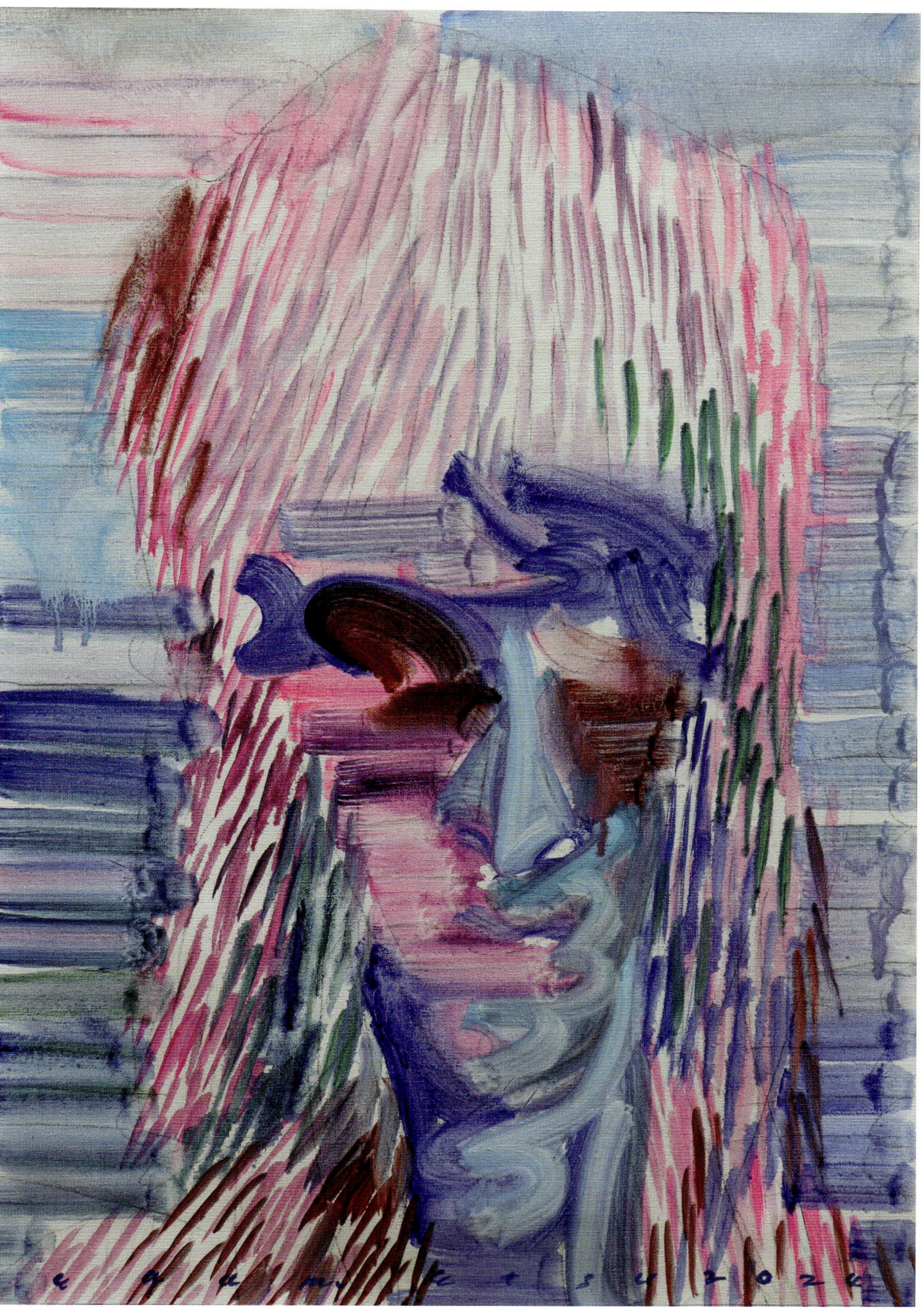

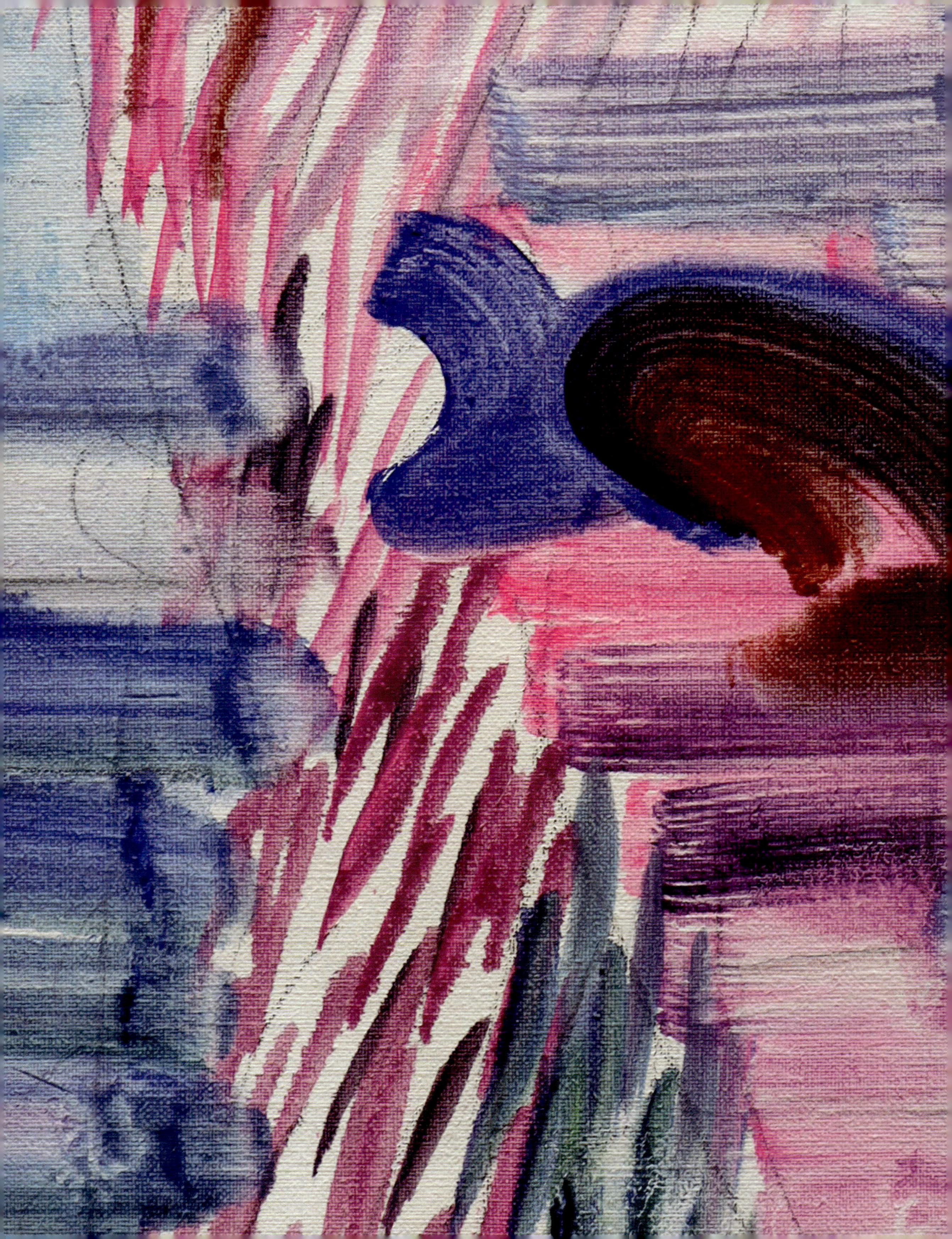

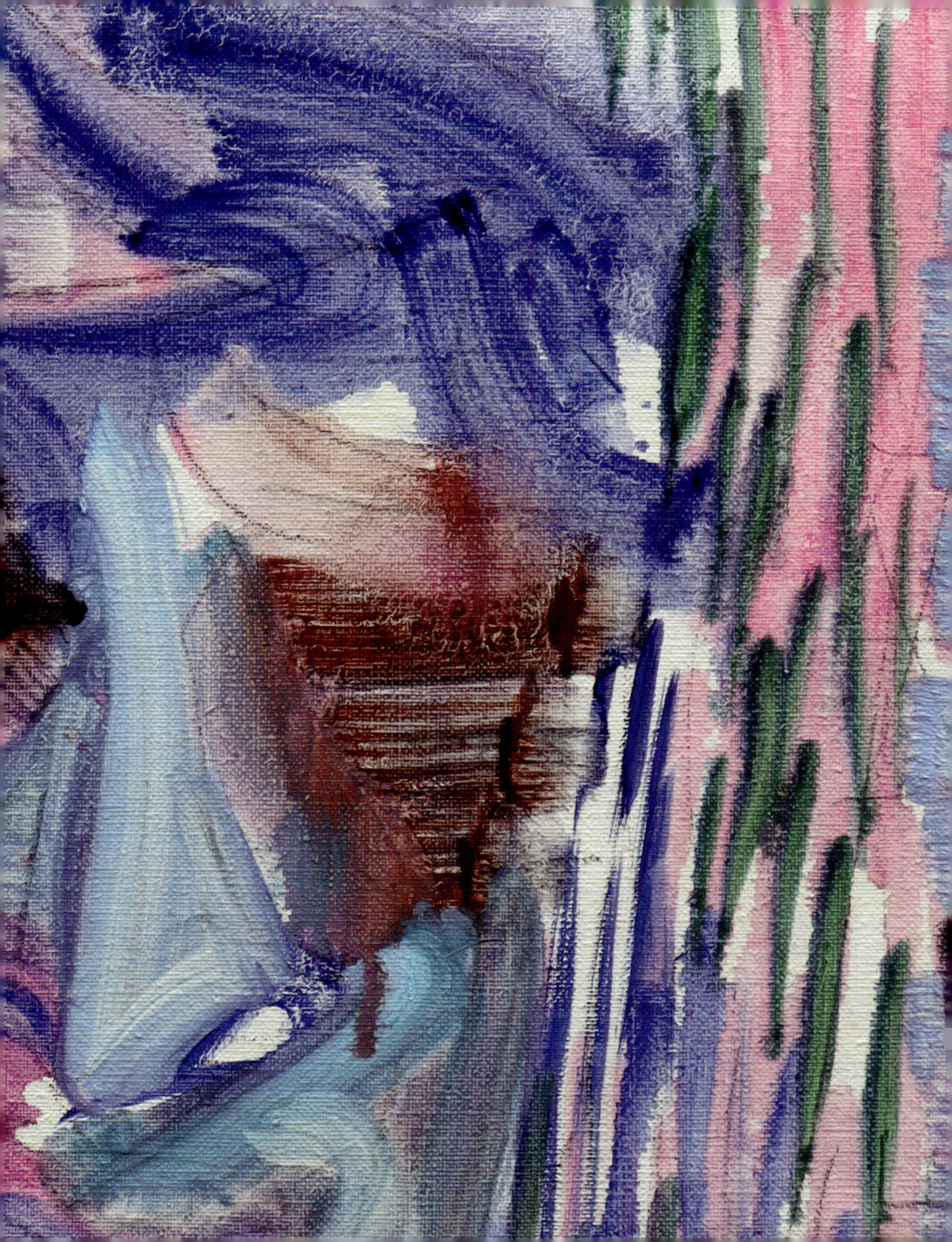

54   RAINBOW – 011, 2024
Oil on canvas / Öl auf Leinwand
27 × 19 ¼ in. / 68,5 × 49 cm

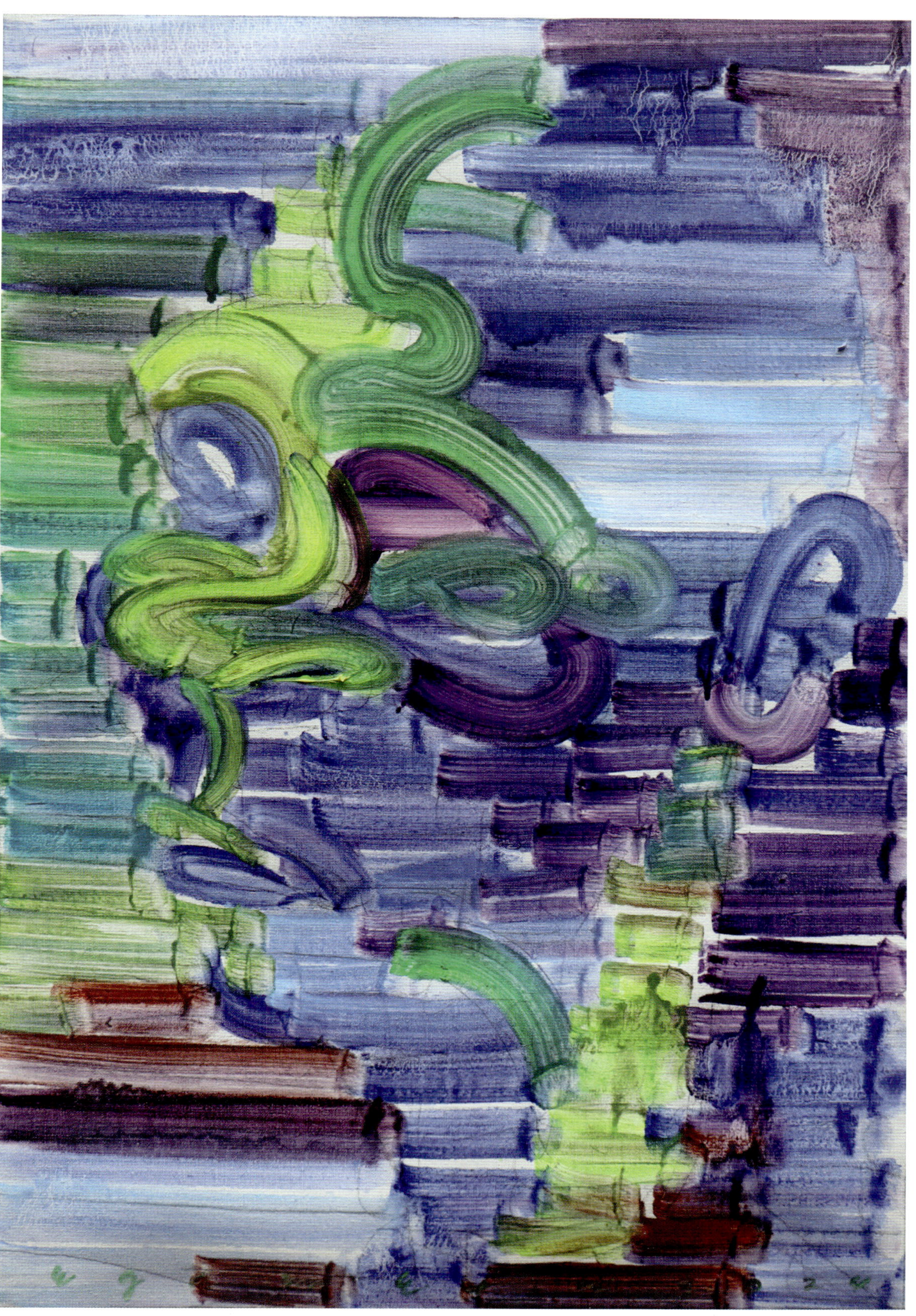

56   RAINBOW – 012, 2024
Oil on canvas / Öl auf Leinwand
27 × 19 ¼ in. / 68,5 × 49 cm

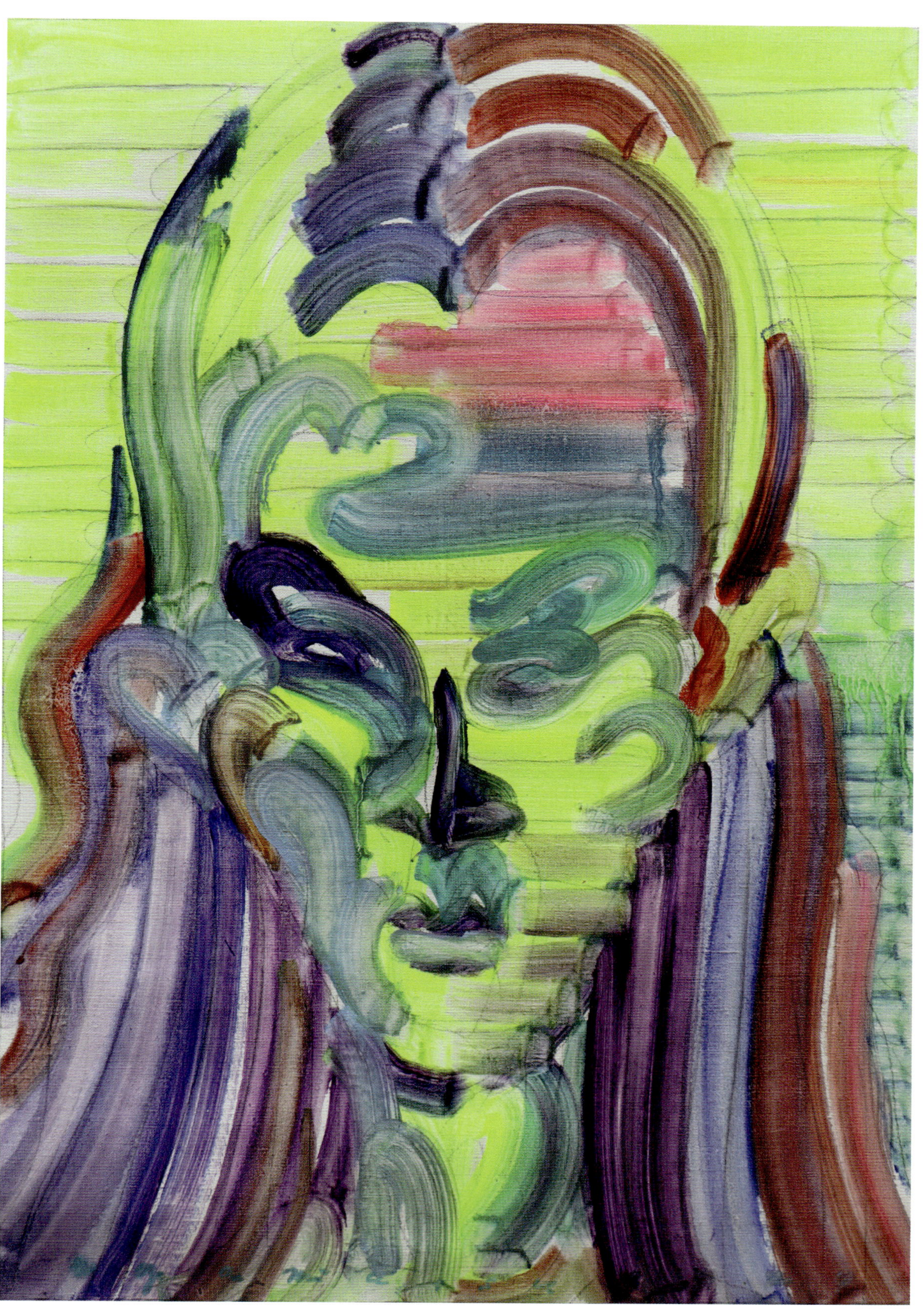

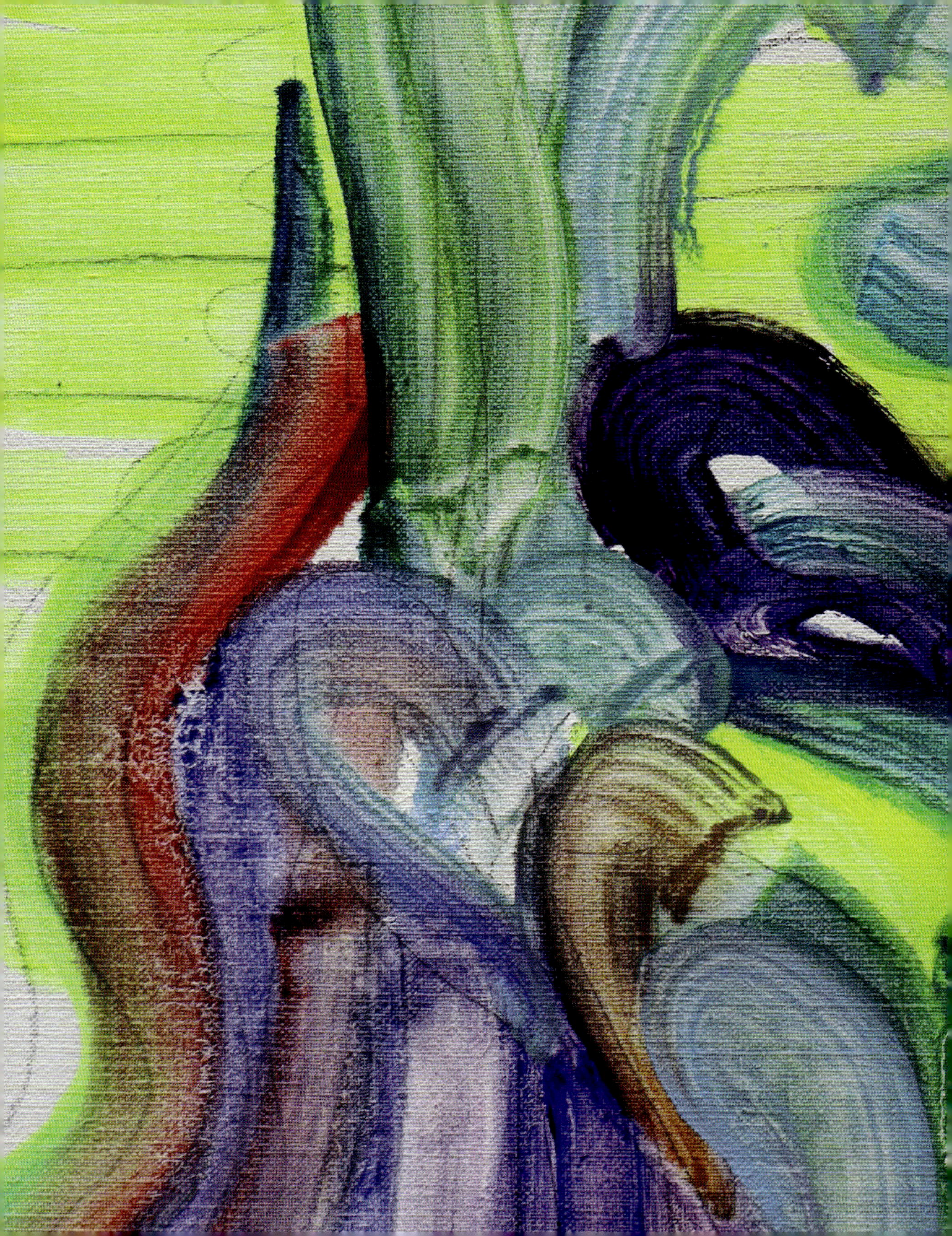

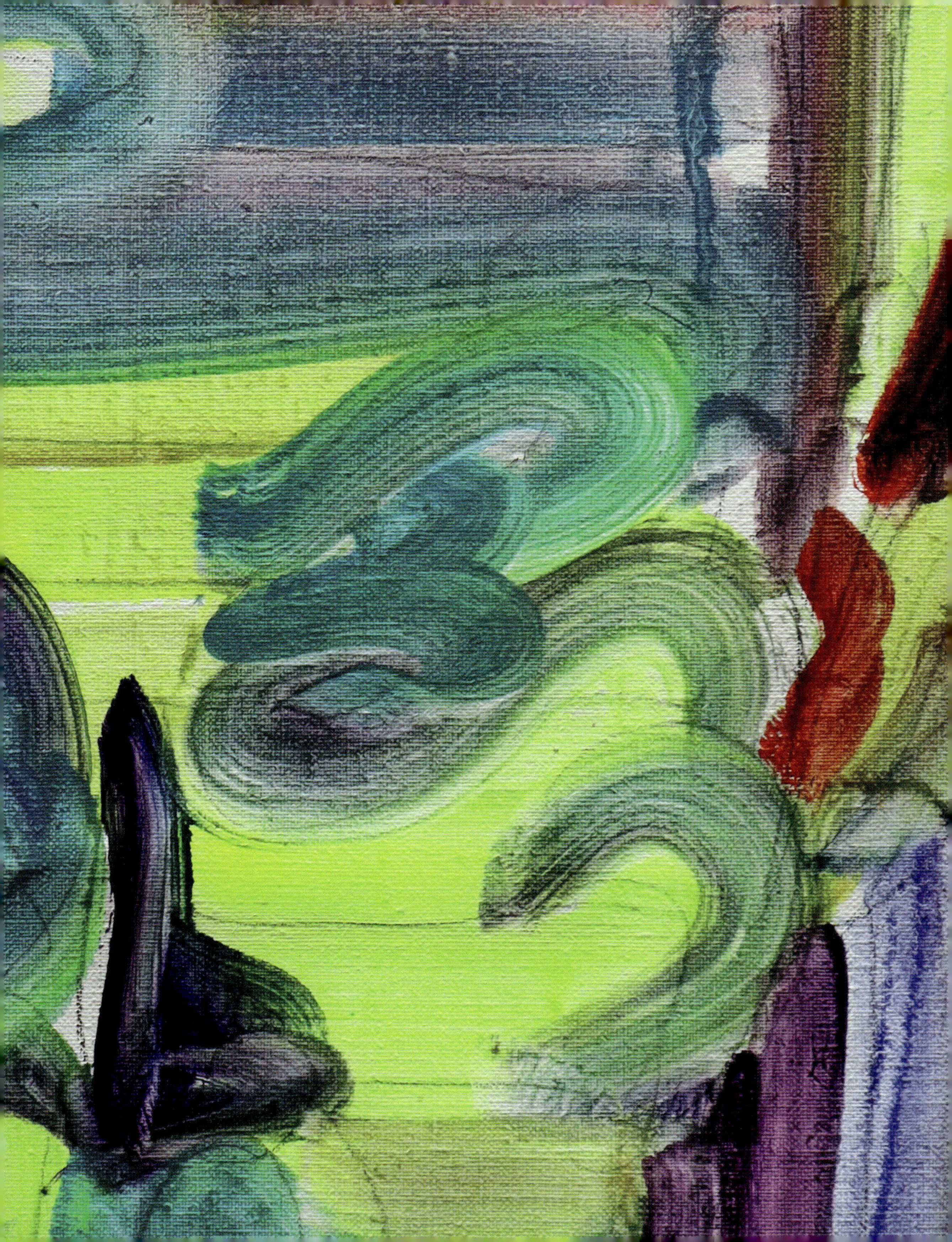

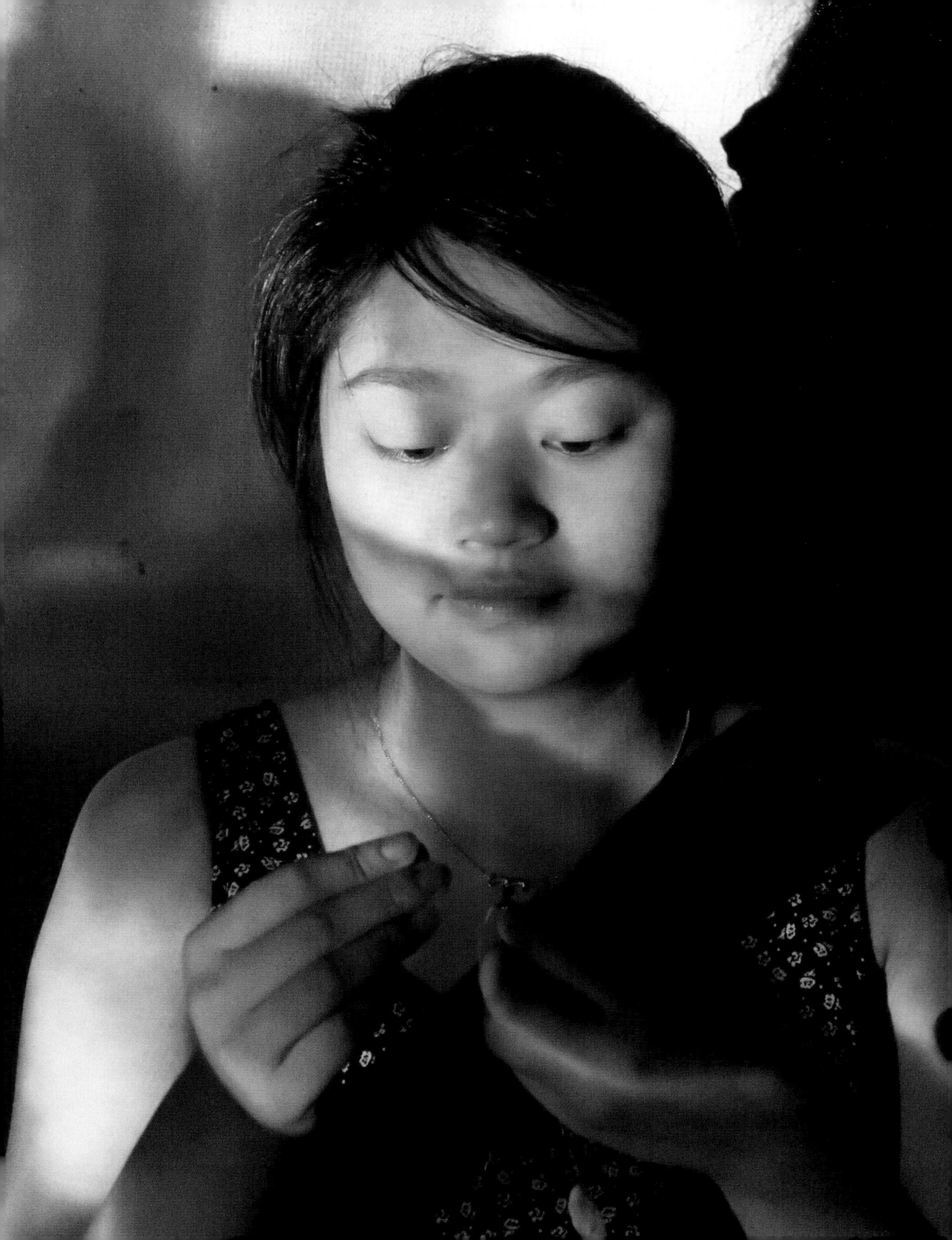

Concise Biography
/ Kurzbiografie

Born in 1994 in Chiba. Etsu Egami lives and works between Tokyo and Beijing, where she is currently pursuing post-doctoral research in art direction at Tsinghua University. She holds a doctorate (2022) and an M.F.A. (2019) from the Central Academy of Fine Arts (CAFA), Beijing, and studied media art at the Karlsruhe University of Arts and Design in Germany (2017).

Geboren 1994 in Chiba. Etsu Egami lebt und arbeitet in Tokio und Peking, wo sie derzeit als Post-Doc an der Tsinghua University im Bereich Art Direction forscht. Sie erlangte einen Doktortitel (2022) und einen M.F.A. (2019) an der Central Academy of Fine Arts (CAFA), Peking, und studierte Medienkunst an der Hochschule für Gestaltung in Karlsruhe (2017).

Selected Solo Exhibitions
/ Ausgewählte Einzelausstellungen

2023	Philosophers, Etsu Egami × JY, Whitestone Gallery H Queen's, Hong Kong
2023	Etsu Egami, Whitestone Gallery, Singapore
2023	Oriental Mystery, HOW Art Museum, Shanghai
2023	Confrontation between instinct and order: Romance of the Three Kingdoms drawn by Egami Etsu, Kyoto Tsutaya Books, Takashimaya Kyoto
2022	Etsu Egami, Obsession and Question, New Horizons of Modern Painting, Woodone Museum of Art, Hiroshima
2022	Did you get it?, Hara Museum ARC, Gunma
2022	Rainbow – Etsu Egami, Tang Contemporary Art, Seoul
2022	Venus Code, A2Z Art Gallery, Paris
2021	Rainbow, Karuizawa New Art Museum, Karuizawa
2021	Facebook, Chambers Fine Art, New York
2021	In a Moment of Misunderstanding, All the Masks Fall, Tang Contemporary Art, Beijing
2021	Star Time, Ginza Six Tsutaya Atrium, Tokyo
2021	Social Distancing, A2Z Art Gallery, Paris
2021	Rainbow, Whitestone Gallery Taipei, Taipei
2020	Entrance Gallery Vol. 1 Egami Etsu, Chiba City Museum of Art, Chiba
2019	Your Name? – Etsu Egami, Whitestone Gallery Ginza, Tokyo
2018	Dialogue beyond 4000 years – Etsu Egami, Chiba Art Center, Chiba
2018	Dialogue beyond 400 years – Etsu Egami, Playground London, London
2017	Into the light…, ßpace, ZKM (Center for Art and Media), Karlsruhe
2016	God's voice, human's words?, DEHAIRI projects, Tokyo
2016	This is Not a Mishearing Game, De Sarthe Gallery, Beijing

Selected Collections
/ Ausgewählte Sammlungen

He Art Museum, Foshan
Yusaku Maezawa Collection, Tokyo
Woodone Museum of Art, Hiroshima
Central Academy of Fine Arts Museum, Beijing
Karuizawa New Art Museum, Karuizawa
Longlati Foundation, Shanghai
Garage Museum of Art, Moscow
Tree Art Museum, Beijing
Yuan Art Museum, Beijing
E-Land Foundation, Seoul
Damei Museum, Beijing
Korea Suncheon Cultural Foundation, Suncheon
Art Collection of Toyama Masamichi (JP)
Nanjo Art Museum, Nanjo
Iris Art Museum, Suzhou
Collection of Joo Hoyoung (SK)
GMO Collection, Tokyo
JINS Collection, Maebashi
Hua Wei Collection, Shenzhen
Art Collection of Kawamura Yoshihisa (JP)
Collection of Mitsubishi Estate Co, Chiyoda
Kiri Capital Collection, Hong Kong

      The Mythenstein Project is a collaboration between ZWEI Wealth and Gerber & Stauffer Fine Arts. Our aim is to offer promising young artists from a wide range of backgrounds the chance to exhibit their work in Switzerland and to make them known to a broader audience than is normally possible in traditional galleries for young art.

As one of the most important marketplaces in the global art trade, Switzerland is a desirable exhibition location for artists at the beginning of their careers, but one that is not easy to access. The Mythenstein Project aims to fill at least a small gap in Switzerland's art infrastructure by making the representative rooms at Villa Mythenstein, the Zurich headquarters of ZWEI Wealth, available to individual artists for a whole year.

Das Mythenstein Project ist eine Kollaboration von ZWEI Wealth und Gerber & Stauffer Fine Arts. Unser Ziel ist es, vielversprechenden jungen Künstlern unterschiedlichster Herkunft eine Ausstellungsplattform in der Schweiz zu bieten und sie einem breiteren Publikum bekannt zu machen, als dies in traditionellen Galerien für junge Kunst normalerweise möglich ist.

Die Schweiz, einer der wichtigsten Kunsthandelsplätze der Welt, gilt als begehrter, doch schwer zugänglicher Ausstellungsort für Künstler*innen zu Beginn ihrer Karriere. Das Mythenstein Project möchte hier eine kleine Lücke in der Schweizer Kunstinfrastruktur schließen, indem wir den eingeladenen Künstler*innen die Repräsentationsräume der Villa Mythenstein, des Zürcher Hauptsitzes von ZWEI Wealth, jeweils für ein ganzes Jahr zur Verfügung stellen.

64

Colophon
/ Impressum

This catalogue is published on the occasion of the exhibition / Dieser Katalog erscheint anlässlich der Ausstellung

Etsu Egami: Rainbow
Villa zum Mythenstein, Zurich / Zürich
5 June 2024–18 April 2025

Editor / Herausgeber
ZWEI Wealth and / und Gerber & Stauffer Fine Arts

ZWEI Wealth AG
Genferstrasse 35
CH-8002 Zurich
www.zwei-wealth.ch

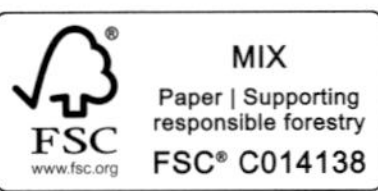

Gerber & Stauffer Fine Arts AG
Langstrasse 151
CH-8004 Zurich
www.gerberstauffer.com

Texts / Texte
Martin Herb, Beate Scheder

Translation / Übersetzung
Nicholas Grindell

Copy editing / Lektorat
Joseph Kuster, Eva Maurer

Design / Gestaltung
BANK™ / www.banktm.de

Image editing / Lithografie
dpi-factory, Krefeld

Production management / Produktion
DCV

Printing and binding / Gesamtherstellung
FINIDR s.r.o., Český Těšín

Copyright
Artworks / Kunstwerke: © the artist, courtesy
Gerber & Stauffer Fine Arts
Portraits of / Portraits von Etsu Egami: © Etsu Egami

This publication is listed in the German National Bibliography by the German National Library. Detailed bibliographic data are available at http://dnb.d-nb.de / Die Deutsche Nationalbibliothek verzeichnet diese Publikation in der Deutschen Nationalbibliografie; detaillierte bibliografische Daten sind im Internet über http://dnb.dnb.de abrufbar.

Distribution and marketing / Vertrieb und Marketing
DCV
sales@dcv-books.com

ISBN 978-3-96912-210-5
Printed in the Czech Republic

Published by / Erschienen bei DCV
www.dcv-books.com

DCV

Project Partners
/ Die Projektpartner

Gerber & Stauffer Fine Arts

Gerber & Stauffer Fine Arts is one of the leading private art dealerships in Switzerland. We advise private and institutional clients in all aspects of building and managing their collections. Acting as agents for our clients or on our own account, we buy and sell important works of art from the late 19th century to the present.

Gerber & Stauffer Fine Arts ist einer der führenden privaten Kunsthändler der Schweiz. Das Unternehmen berät private und institutionelle Kunden in allen Aspekten des Aufbaus und der Verwaltung ihrer Sammlungen. In Vertretung der Kunden oder auf eigene Rechnung erwirbt und verkauft Gerber & Stauffer Fine Arts bedeutende Kunstwerke vom späten 19. Jahrhundert bis zur Gegenwart.

ZWEI Wealth

ZWEI Wealth is a consultancy for wealth planning and management that operates independently of banks, asset managers and other financial service providers. ZWEI Wealth establishes market transparency and effective competition, helps find tailored, individual solutions, as well as sustainably optimising the results. ZWEI Wealth currently operates Europe's largest agency for wealth managers.

ZWEI Wealth ist ein von Banken und Finanzanbietern unabhängiges Beratungsunternehmen für Vermögensplanung und Vermögensverwaltung. ZWEI Wealth etabliert Markttransparenz, effektiven Marktwettbewerb, hilft, individuelle und massgeschneiderte Lösungen zu finden sowie die Ergebnisse nachhaltig zu optimieren. ZWEI Wealth betreibt aktuell die grösste Vermittlungsplattform von Vermögensverwaltern in Europa.